EXPOSED

The world's lies and deceptions uncovered

EXPOSED

The world's lies and deceptions uncovered

EMILY HATFIELD

ISBN-13: 978-0692163405
ISBN-10: 0692163409

Published by The Light Network
TheLightNetwork.tv

Printed in the United States of America

Cover Design: Robert Hatfield
Cover Graphic: Shutterstock.com

To Robert –

Thank you for helping so many of my dreams become realities.
You are my greatest encourager, biggest blessing, and closest friend.

CONTENTS

INTRODUCTION

In the fall of 2008, I was privileged to explore Athens, Rome, Ephesus, Corinth, Crete, and Patmos. The moment I stepped into the ruins of the past, I was changed. Seeing Biblical sites first-hand opens your eyes to Scriptural realities that are easy to miss otherwise. For instance, I never truly appreciated a prison epistle about joy until I stepped into a dark, damp first-century prison. When I returned home from my trip abroad, I knew I had to continue educating myself about first century life.

In 2013, my husband and I traveled back to Greece and Turkey, this time exploring each of the seven churches of Asia as well as other Biblically-significant sites. I didn't know it was possible to fall more in love with first century customs, architecture, and geography, but I did. Upon our return home, I continued my studies of these topics. This book is the product of the passion I cultivated and the knowledge I uncovered while on my journeys abroad.

What struck me most as I visited and studied these ancient sites was the fact that we really neglect to study them as we should. Here were Christians who lived in a world that was extremely ungodly, who faced extreme persecution, and who had oppressive governments. They were wealthy and sophisticated and captivated by material possessions. They were, quite frankly, not that different from us. In fact, their struggles against Satan were exactly the same. Neglecting to study their culture really puts us at a disadvantage. By digging into their first century life, though, we will be better prepared for our own fight against an ungodly culture. After all, times have changed, but the world has not.

In this book we will look at the following tactics that Satan has used and continues to use to deceive Christians: inconvenience, timidity, conformity, idolatry, materialism, persecution, rationalization, complacency, vulnerability, discouragement, distress, and separation.

Each chapter of this book is broken down into three sections: the place, the passage, and the point. In *the place*, you will read a detailed description of the city or region that the chapter is focusing on. Emphasis will be given to pagan worship centers, topography, geography, and other important details specific to each location. *The passage* will highlight one section of scripture written either about the place itself or written to the Christians who lived there. *The point* is just that, a point of application we can glean from our studies. This section will expose Satan's tactics and make a modern application for our fight against him.

It is my prayer that this book will expand your knowledge of first century life, expose the recycled tactics Satan uses to lure Christians away from God, and open your eyes to more Biblical truths that you can apply in your walk with Jesus. We know that Satan is seeking to devour us (1 Pet. 5:8), therefore we must be ready to defend ourselves against his attacks. Since his schemes against mankind today are similar to the schemes he's always used, I pray this book will help you, personally, resist the devil so that he will flee from you (James 4:7).

I

EXPOSING INCONVENIENCE
Asia Minor

*Do you let comfort take precedence
over God's commands?*

⟡

A sia Minor is one of those places in the New Testament that
we read about, perhaps hear about in sermons, yet do not
often take the time to learn anything about its location, culture,
or significance to the first century. It is so easy to skim over
the geographical lists in the Bible, especially if we are wanting
to move on to exciting places like Ephesus and Corinth. Don't
worry, we'll get there. But first, it is helpful to understand the
region that holds so many familiar stories, cities, and faces.
That is why we're going to begin this study by looking into the
place simply known as Asia Minor.

When you read through the New Testament, especially the
book of Acts, and you come to terms like Cappadocia, Pontus,
Bithynia, Galatia, Cilicia, Pamphylia, Lycia, Phrygia, Caria,
Ionia, Lydia, and Mysia, what do you envision? If you're like
I was before traveling to some of these locations, then you
envision nothing. Absolutely nothing. These are just obscure
names that do not really incite much of a reaction. Yet these are
real places. Real people lived there, worked there, and wrestled
with Satan there. For that reason, these places deserve our time
and effort in understanding them because they can teach us

so much when we truly value the geography, topography, and culture of these New Testament places.

That long list of hard-to-pronounce locations? Those are the regions of Asia Minor. It would have consisted of the central and western portions of modern-day Turkey. If you are unfamiliar with the geography of that part of the world, Turkey is just east of Greece. In times just before the New Testament era, the Greeks ruled the world. Even when Rome took over the region in 63 BC, the Greek (Hellenistic) culture still reigned. Since the Greeks watched the sun rise in the east, they called their neighbor *Anatolia*, which means "the land where the sun rises." This name would not be the only Greek influence in Asia Minor, but we will cover that in future chapters.

What, then, was Asia Minor, or Anatolia, like?

When I think of modern-day Turkey, I think of deserts and a very arid climate. This could not be a more inaccurate view of Asia Minor! The land is bordered by many rivers and three seas: the Black Sea (north), the Aegean Sea (west), and the Mediterranean Sea (south). The southern regions of Asia Minor have smooth, fertile soils, warm climates, produce citrus fruits, and are very green. The central and western regions are also lush, though not flat. Instead, there are two major mountain ranges that occupy the area. To the north, the Pontic Mountain Chain, and to the south, the Taurus Mountain Chain. Across the mid-section, the Anatolian Plateau, the area ranges in elevation from 2,000 feet to 4,000 feet west to east. Many of the ancient cities in these regions backed up to beautiful snow-capped mountains while their neighboring cities were low-lying coastal lands. While beautiful, this was not an easy terrain! In fact, Asia Minor's diverse topography was quite inconvenient for those traveling from city to city through various regions.

The cities themselves were also quite fascinating. Having taken on the Hellenistic culture, the inhabitants spoke Koine Greek (one of the most expressive languages in history) and worshiped many Greek gods. However, do not let the proximity to Greece fool you into thinking that the Romans did not have a profound impact on the lives of those in Asia Minor. The Roman roads played a vital role in the prosperity that the region saw in the New Testament time period. Trade routes were established along the thousands of roads the Romans constructed, elevating the profile of coastal cities in the region and bringing more visitors to the area than ever before. Because travel was easier, Asia Minor became a place for Jews to settle after being displaced in 70 AD (when the temple in Jerusalem was destroyed). With these Jewish communities thriving, the gospel was more easily spread in the region and, as we'll see in subsequent chapters, it helped make Asia Minor the hub of this great message.

THE PASSAGE

The Bible gives us our first introduction to Asia Minor in Acts 2, when the Jews gathered on the day of Pentecost from "every nation under heaven" (v. 5). In verses 9 and 10, we have five regions of Asia Minor listed: Cappadocia (Central), Pontus (North), Asia (West), Phrygia (West/Central), and Pamphylia (South). It is likely that at least some of these were among the number converted at the end of the chapter (v. 38), thus paving the way for Christianity in Asia Minor as these new Christians took the message of Jesus back with them.

In Acts 15:41, Paul and Silas departed on their missionary journey and went first through Syria (which borders Turkey on the east) and Cilicia (which is a southern region of Asia Minor) strengthening the churches. Moving into chapter 16, we read that Paul picked up Timothy, whose father was Greek, and took him with him on the journey. Acts 16:4 starts one of those famous lists that we love to skip over, but take a moment to really dive into the text. In verses 6-12, you will read of approximately five regions of Asia Minor that Paul, Silas, and Timothy attempted to go in order to preach the gospel. Five regions! These aren't simply the next 5 exits on the Roman Interstate, these are entire regions! From Acts 15:41 to Acts 16:12, Paul and his companions traveled the entire distance of Asia Minor, which we noted changes in terrain about 2,000 feet in just the middle section! Not to mention, they then traveled across the Aegean Sea into Greece. This would have been a considerable distance, likely around 800 miles[1] (roughly the distance from New York City to Chicago). Notice, though, that this is just the first part of their journey! They will end up going from Greece to Jerusalem, adding another 2,000 miles to the already lengthy trip. Remember, this is just one missionary journey; Paul does three. What great effort!

Acts 19:10 gives us a summary statement of the ministry that went on in this region of the world. The verse says, "all who dwelt in Asia heard the word of the Lord Jesus, both Jews and Greeks." This is just a few short years after the travels from Acts 16, yet the entire area of Asia Minor had received the word of God. There's nothing minor about that!

THE POINT

In seemingly no time at all, the entire area of the world known as Asia Minor heard the word of God. This would have been a difficult feat, especially in an era where there were no planes, cars, or trains. There were no such things as cell phones or Internet access. They didn't even have air conditioning! Yet they expended the necessary effort (and a considerable amount was needed!) to

---

[1] "Paul as Missionary Pastor." *Paul as Missionary: Identity, Activity, Theology, and Practice* (n.d.): n.pag. Web.

spread the gospel message of Jesus Christ. They conquered the rugged, mountainous terrain. They walked mile after mile along the Roman roads. They likely slept where they could and ate where they could. Clearly they were zealous about the work of the Lord, and excited that they were counted worthy to be involved. Because of this, no distance seemed too far; no terrain too difficult. Even when they weren't permitted to go where they wanted (Acts 16:6-7), they went where the Lord would have them go.

Too often, as modern-day Christians, we offer excuses. We don't want to tell our friends, neighbors, or co-workers about Jesus because it might put a strain on our relationship. We don't want to do something as simple as give them a CD or send them an email that will benefit their soul. We think it's difficult, but really, it's not at all. *Difficult* is having to walk up countless hills and mountains. *Difficult* is having to walk everywhere you go. *Difficult* is traveling 800 miles one way, unsure of where you'll sleep or what you'll eat or how the people will receive you. *Difficult* is going all over an entire country only to have your final destination be prison. *Difficult* is what Paul and his companions faced in taking the gospel to all of Asia Minor, and they didn't let that stop them. Instead, they praised God and rejoiced that they were enlisted in His service.

You and I would do well to dwell on the effort it took to take the gospel to all the world in the first century. When we do, maybe we'll stop excusing ourselves or telling ourselves it's too hard for us to do today. Instead, perhaps we'll find the fire and zeal that Paul and others had in taking the gospel to the entire world. When we do, we will see obstacles as opportunities to glorify God. We'll see any amount of effort as the least we could possibly do in response to all Jesus did in coming to earth to die for us. We'll see struggle as a way to share in the sufferings of Christ. After all, that's the way it's intended to be. Evangelism isn't meant to be a chore, it is meant to be a joy. God has entrusted us with His word. Since we are unworthy vessels of such a glorious message, we should gladly and humbly do all that the Lord commands.

Just what does the Lord command when it comes to His saving message? He commands us to share that redemptive story with the world around us (Mark 16:15).

Yes, there will be obstacles in taking that message. However, we cannot let those obstacles keep us from doing what the Lord has commanded. Surely we don't have nearly the amount of obstacles Paul, Silas, and Timothy had, and yet God expected great things of them. And so, in a time when we have every convenience, not to mention the entire gospel plan revealed to us (and likely multiple copies of it in our possession!), let us not slack on our Christian duty. Instead, let us live our lives as Christ (Gal. 2:20), dedicating every part of who we are to His service. His message to us, individually, is to take the message that has changed our lives and our very eternity to those around us. Take it excitedly! Take it unapologetically! Just take it! Sow the seed, and God will give the increase (1 Cor. 3:6).

There are many ways this can be accomplished, and we will not all do it the same way. God has given each of us unique talents and abilities, as well as unique platforms. You have a set of friends and family members with whom I may never come in contact. Perhaps you have a blog, a large Twitter or Instagram following, or hundreds of friends on Facebook. Maybe you are a staple figure in your community. It could be that you have a job that frequently puts you in the public eye. In whatever place you find yourself, let God use you as the vessel He created you to be (2 Cor. 4:7).

> For we are His workmanship, created in Christ Jesus for good works, which God prepared beforehand that we should walk in them (Eph. 2:10).

The word translated "workmanship" literally means "the product of His hand." God is truly the Potter and we are the clay

(Isa. 64:8). Let Him mold you for good works. Let Him use your life, your influence, and your position for His glory. Let Him use you to reach the lost people He loves so much. God has placed the beautiful message of His Beloved Son into your hands, and He has blessed you to live in an age where it's easier than ever to spread it! Don't offer excuses as to why evangelism is too difficult. Don't complain that you aren't equipped with the same talents as so-and-so. While we are all different, we are all required to be busy about our Father's business. Even if you consider yourself a one-talent man, you are still to do more with that talent than bury it in the sand (Mat. 25:24-25).

Evangelism has never been easy, but it has always been necessary. Instead of focusing on the difficulty, focus on very real, dedicated men of faith like Paul, Silas, and Timothy. Ask God to give you the same zeal that carried these men hundreds of miles and over difficult terrain. Thank God for blessing you with modern conveniences and abilities, and beg Him to help you never use those blessings as excuses.

If the people in the first century could take the gospel to an entire region without the use of email or cell phones or cars or television, truly we are without excuse in an age where you have to try to get away from some form of communication. Don't let Satan's whisper of *"it's too hard"* keep you from being involved in the greatest work on earth. After all, it is within the context of evangelism that Jesus promises to be with us always (Mat. 28:20). With Him, we can do all things (Phi. 4:13).

⁊⁘⁖

I.   How do you think Paul cultivated the zeal he had for the work of the Lord?

II. What modern comforts do you have that could aid you in evangelism?

III. If Paul were alive today, do you think he would use social media to spread the gospel? How might he do that? How can you implement these tactics in your outreach?

IV. What excuses do you offer for not being more evangelistic?

V.   In what specific ways can you carry out the great commission (Mat. 28:18-20)? List specific people you want to reach this month.

II

EXPOSING TIMIDITY
Athens

Will you stand up or be silent when God's message is unpopular?

❧

Throughout history, Athens, Greece has been a prominent city. Established somewhere between 1600-1200 BC, the city saw many ups and downs throughout the centuries. With its desirable location near the sea and its high acropolis, Athens was attacked numerous times by military giants seeking to increase their borders. For the most part, though, Athens was able to hold its own; that is, until the Roman empire came into power. Fortunately, the city officials made some very wise decisions during this time and formed an alliance with the military powerhouse, leading Rome to show Athens special treatment in the years to come. Unfortunately, Athens turned away from their ally in a rebellion, and Rome stripped the renowned city of its military and political power, though it did show mercy in letting the city remain "a university town and center of culture, philosophy, and education."[1]

While Athens would lose its political influence, its cultural influence remained strong. Rome might have been unmatched in power, but they could not overtake the Greek culture. Thus,

---

[1] Fant, Clyde E., and Mitchell Glenn Reddish. *A Guide to Biblical Sites in Greece and Turkey.* New York: Oxford UP, 2003. Print. 14

Koine Greek was the common language of the day instead of Latin. Furthermore, wealthy Roman citizens "sent their children to Athens to be educated by its philosophers and gain sophistication in the presence of its culture."[2] Rome was mighty while Athens was prestigious.

Two such groups of philosophical influence that made Athens their home were the Stoics and Epicureans. The Stoics were known for reason, claiming that the highest level of human satisfaction came from rationality. Their entire lives were dedicated to the pursuit of reason. Epicureans, on the other hand, believed everything in the world existed for the mere satisfaction of the individual. Their entire lives were dedicated to the pursuit of pleasure.

Due to the eclectic nature of the citizens of Athens, the city had numerous outlets for worship. Most notable was the temple of Athena, commonly called the Parthenon. Built in 432 bc, the Parthenon stood atop the Athenian acropolis in a mighty and noteworthy fashion. The building itself was gorgeous: outside, beautiful friezes (large, horizontal bands of sculpted decor) that depicted many mythological stories; inside, a gilded statue of the goddess Athena that stood at a towering 40 feet (roughly the height of a three-story home).

Surrounding the acropolis were many other temples of worship. The Greek deities Zeus, Ares, Hephaestus, and Aphrodite all had temples dedicated to them. Though it was only a city of approximately 20,000-25,000 residents, there was no shortage of magnificent structures, each a testimony to the cultural and religious prestige for which Athens was renowned.

Resting just below the acropolis and in the shadow of the majestic Parthenon was a rocky hill known as the Areopagus, also referred to as Mars Hill. This is where philosophers brought

---

[2] *Ibid.,* 12.

the apostle Paul in order that they might "hear something new" (Acts 17:21). The Bible tells us that there were more areas of worship located here (Acts 17:23), though the Areopagus was primarily used as a public forum. It is fitting, then, that the apostle Paul would deliver such a passionate sermon to the residents of Athens in this notable location.

THE PASSAGE

We read in Acts 17:14 that Paul was sent to Athens alone, leaving his companions Silas and Timothy behind in Berea. While other Christians accompanied him to the famous city, it appears they left him rather quickly in order to retrieve his comrades so that they might all be reunited as a preaching team once again (v. 15). While waiting, Paul began preaching and teaching. For the Jews, he used the synagogue; the Gentiles, the agora (or marketplace). On one such occasion, while speaking in the agora, Paul encountered Stoic and Epicurean philosophers who were quite intrigued by what he had to say. Some scoffed, but others appeared genuinely interested in the peculiar message about "Jesus and the resurrection" (Acts 17:18). For this reason, they invited him away from the marketplace and onto Mars Hill so they could learn more about this strange new doctrine.

Paul, never one to back away from an opportunity to preach the gospel, stood boldly in front of the assembly and delivered a magnificent monologue about Almighty God.

Men of Athens, I perceive that in all things you are very religious; for as I was passing through and considering the objects of your worship, I even found an altar with this inscription: TO THE UNKNOWN GOD. Therefore, the One whom you worship without knowing, Him I proclaim to you: God, who made the world and everything in it, since He is Lord of heaven and earth, does not dwell in temples made with hands. Nor is He worshiped with men's hands, as though He needed anything, since He gives to all life, breath, and all things. And He has made from one blood every nation of men to dwell on all the face of the earth, and has determined their pre-appointed times and the boundaries of their dwellings, so that they should seek the Lord, in the hope that they might grope for Him and find Him, though He is not far from each one of us; for in Him we live and move and have our being, as also some of your own poets have said, "For we are also His offspring." Therefore, since we are the offspring of God, we ought not to think that the Divine Nature is like gold or silver or stone, something shaped by art and man's devising. Truly, these times of ignorance God overlooked, but now commands all men everywhere to repent, because He has appointed a day on which He will judge the world in righteousness by the Man whom He has ordained. He has given assurance of this to all by raising Him from the dead (Acts 17:22-31).

This sermon is remarkably powerful in and of itself. Simply sitting back and soaking in all of the truths about God can leave you speechless and in complete awe. Yet, the true beauty of this passage is lost without considering the location of the speech. Remember that the Areopagus rests just below the massive, ornate, highly esteemed Parthenon -- home to the 40-foot goddess Athena. On every side, there were temples and shrines to false gods. In the shadow of these grand structures and in the very midst of an abundance of pagan worship, Paul boldly declared: God does not live in temples like these. God is not in the Parthenon. God is not shaped by man's hands. God is above all and through all and in all, so repent of your wickedness and turn to Him.

Wow! Paul had some serious gumption.
The question is, do we?

THE POINT

Being a disciple of Jesus means having boldness. It means looking around at your present world and being stirred to action. Acts 17:16 says that Paul's "spirit was provoked within him when he saw that the city was given over to idols." Of course it was! The very name of the city was derived from the false goddess Athena. Yet Paul didn't simply sit back and say, "Well, that's just how it's going to be." Paul was an advocate for change. He knew that the change this city needed could only come from Jesus Christ. Since He had the message of Christ within him, he could spark a change in the people around him. It simply took standing up and speaking out.

When was the last time your spirit was provoked because of all the wickedness surrounding you? When were you last stirred to speak because those around you seemed ignorant of God and all He had done for them? Maybe you cannot recall the last time such a feeling came over you. Maybe we have all become calloused to how much immorality is around us at any given moment. If that is the case, we need to open our eyes. We need to look at the lost and dying world around us and really see them. See their final destination. See the anguish that awaits them. See the severity of their actions, then be moved with compassion to do something - say something - about it.

We know that Jesus was provoked to action when He saw the wickedness of the money changers in the temple (Mat. 21:12-13). Paul would continually speak out when things were amiss, both here on Mars Hill and in the letters he sent to erring congregations. Truly the two were kindred spirits. Since we are to follow their examples (1 Cor. 11:1), it seems our spirits need to be stirred. We need to be shaken out of our timid, fearful state and have the fire reignited in our very souls.

It won't be easy, living this way. It will require a lot of effort on our part. It will take standing in direct opposition to popular opinion. Paul stood with his back to one of the most famous buildings in the world and said, "God does not dwell in temples made with hands" (Acts 17:24). In a city that boasted about their statue of Athena that was covered in 44 talents of gold, Paul says, "we ought not to think that the Divine Nature is like gold or silver or stone, something shaped by art and man's devising" (v. 29). Would this have been a well-received ideology? Unlikely. Still, Paul knew that he needed to speak the truth, regardless of if it was "in season or out of season" (2 Tim. 4:2).

Sometimes, though, we lack the motivation to stand up for the truth because we don't have the knowledge to back it up. Yes, Paul had worldly knowledge of different poets and different philosophies, likely because his hometown of Tarsus was also a major center for philosophy. But forget worldly knowledge and statistics for a moment. Isn't it the case that sometimes we don't even have the biblical knowledge we need? We don't know where certain passages are found so we don't want to mention that the Bible speaks against a certain lifestyle or action. We are unclear about what certain parts of the Bible even mean, so we excuse ourselves from boldly proclaiming God's message. These aren't excuses, just shameful realities. How can we take the word of God boldly to our fellow man when we don't even have it hidden in our own hearts? It's impossible!

God has chosen preaching as the means through which His message is to be carried to the world. We are the vessels who have been entrusted with His precious, soul-saving truth. If we shirk our responsibility to hide His word in our hearts, shame on us! We are not only disappointing and failing our God, we are utterly failing our fallen world. "How then shall they call on Him in whom they have not believed? And how shall they believe in Him of whom they have not heard? And how shall they hear without a preacher?" (Rom. 10:14).

We are His workmanship. We are the feet and the hands that do the work of our Lord. If we are unwilling to go, to speak, to do...who will? Who will go? Who will speak? Who will do? The world is not going to become less vocal. Immorality is not going to cease on its own. Values that the world holds dear are not going to somehow turn themselves around. These things must be taught. These lessons must be learned from God. We are His messengers, and if we fail to view ourselves as such, the entire world will continue in a miserable state of existence.

Paul, alone in a foreign city, was stirred to speak out against the immorality surrounding him. He spoke boldly, making no excuse for the truth, but simply laying it out for others to take for themselves. This is our job. We are the sowers, taking God's message wherever we go. We do so boldly and unapologetically, just as the apostle Paul did, taking the entire message of God to the lost world. We don't merely give them snippets that are the most palatable; we give them the whole truth about who God is, what His Son has done, and where a life lived in sin will lead. If we don't, these people will have no chance of coming to know the God of all grace and mercy and forgiveness. But if we will – if we'll let the word of God and our love for Him stir us to action – perhaps we'll be able to forever alter the course of someone's life, just as Paul did for those who believed that fateful day on Mars Hill (Acts 17:34).

Remember, though, that Paul was bold while still speaking the truth in love. He never argued for the sake of arguing, nor did he use the gospel as a hammer, beating people into submission. My good friend Christy Jenkins once said, "Paul was bold without being brash; he was unapologetic without being insulting. Nobody was ever won to the gospel through obnoxious behavior." We must never use our platform (regardless of how large or small it may be) to speak in a way that is not Christlike. Every interaction we have with the lost should be motivated by love. Every word that we speak should be "seasoned with salt" (Col. 4:6). Our conversations ought to be powerful, yet peaceable; without hesitation, but with all humility; full of Biblical principles while also full of grace.

᷈ᷜᷚ

I: Where was the Areopagus in relation to the Parthenon?

II: List the specific things from the following verses of Acts 17 that Paul was combatting in Athens:

Verse 24 - temples made with hands:

_____

Verse 29 - Divine Nature is not like silver or gold or stone:

_____

III: What excuses do you offer for not speaking boldly about the Word of God?

IV: With what portions of the Bible do you need more familiarization?

V: What types of things in the present world should provoke us to action?

EXPOSING
CONFORMITY
Corinth

*Do you want to look like
the culture or the Christ?*

⊱⊰

The city of Corinth is located on an isthmus in southern Greece, connecting the two mainland peninsulas of the country. It is surrounded by fertile plains and natural springs, and throughout the ages has been quite a city of commerce and prosperity. Originally settled around 4000 BC, Corinth saw many turnovers in ownership due to its central location between military powerhouses Athens and Sparta. During the time of the Roman empire's invasion of the area, General Lucius Mummius completely obliterated the city, tearing down its walls, looting, then burning anything that was left. Most of the residents fled, and the ones who remained were either executed or sold into slavery.

In 46 BC, Julius Caesar reestablished the city as a Roman colony, filling it with Italians and Greeks. "One estimate places the population of Corinth as one-third freemen, one-third slaves, and one-third freedmen (or emancipated slaves)."[1] While this brought a lot of diversity to Corinth, it also brought a lot of hostility between the classes. The majority of the

---

[1] Fant, Clyde E., and Mitchell Glenn Reddish. *A Guide to Biblical Sites in Greece and Turkey*. New York: Oxford UP, 2003. Print. 48

freedmen took up jobs as merchants since they had likely been trained in similar areas of work by their former masters; however, these working class individuals were regarded as the low-lifes of society by those who had always been free.

Quite a few of those in the working class rose to considerable wealth, though, due to the flourishing commerce of the city. Since Corinth was nestled in a key location, with a port on the west that connected them with Italy and a port on the east that connected them with Asia Minor, the city saw extreme wealth because of its exports. One of the most notable exports was Corinthian bronze. Said to be of even more value than gold or silver, this precious metal even lined one of the gates of Jerusalem.

Tourism also brought money to the city. The Isthmian games, established in 582 BC, were held in Corinth every two years and attracted thousands of visitors. These games, second only to the Olympic games, lasted for weeks and brought people from all over the region to the bustling city. With Rome supporting most of the efforts of their newly established colony, Corinth quickly overshadowed its neighbor Athens and grew to fame seemingly overnight.

With fame, money, and an influx of visitors, it is no surprise that Corinth was also known as a city of moral depravity. As early as the fourth century BC, "whenever a playwright wished to depict a drunk on stage, he was always shown wearing a Corinthian hat."[2] Perhaps some of the immorality of the city could be linked to the amount of sailors coming in and out of the ports and the amount of prostitution that was associated with such. There was also an abundance of idolatry in the city, with a world-renowned temple dedicated to the goddess

---

[2] Fant, Clyde E., and Mitchell Glenn Reddish. *A Guide to Biblical Sites in Greece and Turkey*. New York: Oxford UP, 2003. Print. 13

of love, Aphrodite, located on the city's acropolis. There were various other temples as well: the Temple of Apollo, erected in 550 BC, the temple dedicated to Caesar Augustus' sister, Octavia, and one for Asclepius, the god of healing.

With an abundance of wealth, moral degradation, and a host of other temptations surrounding them on literally every side, it is no wonder the Christians in Corinth were called to be a people who were different than their surroundings.

THE PASSAGE

From the outset of 1 Corinthians, Paul appeals to the church's sanctification (1:2). These Christians struggled to get the world out of their hearts so that Jesus could abide there. Paul clues us in on the reason they were struggling; it was because they had been previously involved in very different lifestyles. The majority of these converts in Corinth weren't Jews who had been living in a relatively moral way their entire lives; these were unchurched Gentiles whose only real exposure to religion was founded on prostitution, votive offerings, and fulfilling one's own lusts. Here were people who had once been fornicators, idolators, adulterers, homosexuals, sodomites, thieves, covetous, drunkards, revilers, and extortioners (1 Cor. 6:9-10), yet they had been called out of these lifestyles and "washed, sanctified, and justified in the name of the Lord Jesus Christ" (v. 11).

Those are two extremes, so it's no wonder these people struggled with truly being new in Christ. Still, the apostle Paul commanded them to be a holy people. He did not excuse their backgrounds. Instead, he saw them as those who had been bought with the precious blood of Jesus and were now held to a higher standard than the rest of the world. They were to be different, even if it was difficult. Thus the books of 1st and 2nd

Corinthians address the different issues that this congregation faced as they journeyed toward that end.

Here were Christians who had been condoning – if not celebrating – immorality not even named among the Gentiles (1 Cor. 5:1-2). They had aligned themselves under men instead of under Christ (1 Cor. 1:12-13). They competed for and were jealous of each other's spiritual gifts (1 Cor. 12). They behaved as "mere men" (1 Cor. 3:3). So, in 2 Corinthians 6:11-7:1, Paul addressed the need for the Corinthians' new, holy lifestyle:

> O Corinthians! We have spoken openly to you, our heart is wide open. You are not restricted by us, but you are restricted by your own affections. Now in return for the same (I speak as to children), you also be open. Do not be unequally yoked together with unbelievers. For what fellowship has righteousness with lawlessness? And what communion has light with darkness? And what accord has Christ with Belial? Or what part has a believer with an unbeliever? And what agreement has the temple of God with idols? For you are the temple of the living God. As God has said: "I will dwell in them and walk among them. I will be their God, and they shall be My people." Therefore "Come out from among them, and be separate, says the Lord. Do not touch what is unclean, and I will receive you. I will be a Father to you, and you shall be My sons and daughters, Says the Lord Almighty." Therefore, having these promises, beloved, let us cleanse ourselves from all filthiness of the flesh and spirit, perfecting holiness in the fear of God."

While the Corinthians might have been less familiar with Almighty God than their Jewish brothers and sisters, they were very familiar with temples. Paul told these Christians that it was not the magnificent, ancient structures that housed God, but it was, in fact, their own hearts. This would have resonated with a people surrounded by pagan practices and monumental temples. It would have changed everything in their approach to living a godly life.

THE POINT

Regardless of your background – whether you grew up exposed to God or not – when you became a Christian you were called to a new standard. You were called out of darkness and into His marvelous light (1 Pet. 2:9). You were simply called *out:* out of the world, out of cultural norms, out of self-fulfillment and pleasure. When you submitted to Christ in baptism, you put to death the old man and his deeds (Col. 3:9) and became a new creature, one who lives his or her entire life dedicated to fulfilling God's will. It's all about coming out from the world and being separate, cleansing yourself of the filth of the flesh and striving for holiness (2 Cor. 7:1).

Sometimes, though, it is difficult to get the world out. We get most of the world out, and feel pretty good about it. The reality is, being truly set apart doesn't mean getting away from *most* sin. It means there is a clean break. You can't ride the line and be truly separate from the world. You can't participate in less immorality than you used to and call yourself clean. To be wholly sanctified means you rid yourself of all iniquity and strive for a life of complete purity in Jesus, letting His blood cleanse you when you fall short.

The Corinthians would have understood the sacred nature of the temples around them. There were priests and priestesses serving in them, a grand majority of whom would have been virgins, seeking to keep themselves undefiled in the presence of a pagan deity. There were different rituals that had to be performed in order to keep the temples acceptable before its patron god or goddess. The Corinthians understood this. What they did not seem to comprehend was that *they* were the temple of the living God (1 Cor. 3:17). *They* were to be kept pure and undefiled. *They* were to be presented before God as holy. It was not about the building in which they worshiped Him; it was about *them*.

In today's society, we seem to forget these same things. We place too much significance on the literal structure where we worship, making sure we always say the right things and wear the right things when we're inside of the building, as if it's a holy place. But the place isn't holy! What's holy are the people – the temples of God – and that holiness is to be present both within the worship assembly and without. We are called to be a holy people twenty-four hours a day, seven days a week.

Just as the Corinthian Christians struggled to keep the world's influence out of their hearts and out of the assembly, so too do we. We bicker and complain when certain people are chosen to fulfill special roles within the congregation. We compete for areas of prominence, instead of humbling ourselves and seeking to serve and love one another with all of our might (1 Cor. 12-13). We view each other by social status and race, rather than understanding that we are all one in Christ (1 Cor. 12:12-13). We elevate preachers and preaching styles above our Lord, then let our opinions on such trivial things cause division (1 Cor. 1:10-15). We overlook iniquity in our congregations because we don't want to offend anyone by calling out sin, instead of purging wickedness from among us in order to keep the bride of Christ pure (1 Cor. 5:11-13). We puff ourselves up when dealing with a weaker brother, instead of doing everything within our power to keep from being a stumbling block (1 Cor. 8:10-13). These are things that worldly people do, not people who have been separated for God's holy purpose.

Paul tells the Corinthians, "if anyone is in Christ, he is a new creation: old things have passed away; behold, all things have become new" (2 Cor. 5:17). While your previous life was spent self-seeking, your new life is spent Christ-seeking. Your past life was all about pursuing pleasure; your new life is about pursuing purity. Do not let our adversary, Satan, deceive you into thinking you don't have to be that different as a Christian.

That is a lie! Everything about you must change when you become a Christian. Otherwise, why did Jesus die? Why did He go through the cruel scourging and endless taunts if people could just remain the same; if they could simply become slightly better versions of the people they already were? In light of all that Christ went through, it is nothing for us to change all of who we are! It is nothing to become completely different than the world around us – the world that put Him on the cross.

The world that the Corinthian Christians were living in was an immoral one. The city was laden with every type of wickedness. If their call was still holiness, so is ours. Regardless of the state our society gets to, we are to be different. Regardless of the moral decline the world sinks into, we are to be separate. Fortunately for us, the more wicked the world becomes, the more distinct Christ's bride can be. But notice that the church can be more distinct only if its members remember that they are the temples of God and they are the ones called to be completely different than the world around them.

∂∞∾

I: List the types of things in which the Corinthian Christians were once involved (1 Cor. 6:9-10).

II: What changed (1 Cor. 6:11)?

III: In what ways does worldliness creep into your congregation?

IV: In what ways does worldliness creep into your heart?

V: Write 2 Corinthians 5:17 and place it somewhere you will see it. It might be most helpful to place it somewhere that is close to a temptation to be like the world (e.g. computer, television, closet, etc.).

IV

EXPOSING IDOLATRY
Ephesus

*Do you serve your own
lusts or the Lord?*

⊱⊰

Ephesus is one of the most spectacular places to visit in Asia Minor, and it seemingly always has been. As a port city, Ephesus saw many visitors throughout its impressive history, though the port wasn't the only draw for such a magnificent place. During the reign of Augustus (the time of Christ), Ephesus was said to be the most important city in all of Asia Minor and the fourth most important city in all of the Roman world. One reason for this was that Ephesus was home to one of the seven wonders of the ancient world: the Artemisium.

The Artemisium, or Temple of Artemis (Greek goddess of hunting), was the largest religious building in the known world, boasting 127 massive columns and coming in at approximately four times the size of the Parthenon in Athens, Greece. Originally constructed sometime around the eighth century BC, the Temple of Artemis saw many reconstructions throughout the years due to fires, earthquakes, and conquering kings. During the New Testament era (and the time Paul would have lived in the city), the Artemisium was on its fifth rebuild, but the building remained quite impressive. Thousands traveled to Ephesus each spring as part of a pilgrimage dedicated to

Artemis, and the city became known as (and even boasted about being) the temple keeper of the goddess.

The Artemisium was the most notable temple in Ephesus, but not the only one. There were dozens of temples lining the agoras (marketplaces) and marble streets of this monumental city. Imperial worship (worship of Roman emperors) was a common practice in Ephesus, with Domitian and Hadrian each having temples dedicated to them. One of the gates in the city was dedicated to Augustus and even called him a "son of a god." Clearly, this city was running rampant with idolatry.

Beyond the temples, there were other impressive structures in the city, the most famous likely being the theater. Completed in 54 AD, the grand theater in Ephesus had around 24,500 seats (comparable to Rupp Arena, the largest indoor arena in the United States) and some of the most amazing acoustics in the world. With thousands of seats towering around you, if you stand in the center of the theater and simply whisper, even those in the top rows are able to hear you perfectly. Thus, this theater was used for plays, civic meetings, concerts, and other events that you would expect such a large venue to hold. It would have also had some of involvement with the pilgrimages that people took to the temple of Artemis. There is an inscription near the south entrance of the theater that depicts a processional along what was called the Sacred Way, which led visitors right by the theater and toward the grand Artemisium.

No matter the types of things in which you were involved, you could not help but be surrounded by larger than life structures in the city of Ephesus. But, you also could not escape the idolatry that permeated the very core of this impressive and influential city.

THE PASSAGE

In Acts 19 we are introduced to Paul's time in the city of Ephesus. He begins by teaching in the synagogue (a common first stop for Paul in new cities) for three months (v. 8), but not all were receiving him well. So, he went to the school of Tyrannus and continued his teaching there for two years (v. 9). While living and teaching in Ephesus, Paul did many miracles and converted many souls to Jesus, a large portion of whom had previously been sorcerers (involved in false magic) and idolaters. This was an amazing boost for the cause of Christ, but it was detrimental to those who made their profits selling things that related to magic and, most especially, the goddess Artemis.

Acts 19:24 introduces us to a silversmith named Demetrius who made his money off relics dedicated to the goddess Artemis. Due to his lagging profits, he decided to start a commotion about Christianity, inciting a violent herd mentality along the way. He called together others of his trade and gave a diatribe against Paul and "the Way" about which he was preaching. Verses 25-27 give us his speech:

> Men, you know that from this business we have our wealth. And you see and hear that not only in Ephesus but in almost all of Asia this Paul has persuaded and turned away a great many people, saying that gods made with hands are not gods. And there is danger not only that this trade of ours may come into disrepute but also that the temple of the great goddess Artemis may be counted as nothing, and that she may even be deposed from her magnificence, she whom all Asia and the world worship (ESV).

The response was immediate: "Great is Artemis of the Ephesians!" The men let their wrath get the best of them and they rushed toward the grand theater, chanting and stirring up the crowds as they went. On the way, they grabbed some of Paul's companions and hauled them into the theater with the vengeful, screaming crowd. Due to the violent nature of the whole ordeal, some of the disciples restrained Paul from going to the theater, fearing what may happen to him if he did (Acts 19:30-31). By the time the masses entered the theater, half of them did not even know why they were there; they were simply screaming for the sake of screaming. Alexander motioned for the crowd to be quiet so he could make a defense, yet when they found out he was a Jew they shouted for two solid hours, "Great is Artemis of the Ephesians!" (Acts 19:34).

Finally, a city clerk was able to quiet the crowd and then gave a very politically charged speech in which he urged Demetrius and the others to take their complaints to the proconsuls (military commanders). He satisfied the idolatrous crowd by stroking their ego, mentioning that everyone in all of Asia knew of Ephesus as the temple keeper of the "great goddess" Artemis. This seemed to appease the crowd and they dispersed. While this is the end of the account in the Scriptures, we know that this wasn't the end of Artemis pride in the city of Ephesus, and likely was only the beginning of the difficulty Christians would face as they opposed such highly esteemed Ephesian values.

THE POINT

A lot of what is happening in Acts 19 seems positive. Because of Paul's preaching and the heart of the listeners, the business of Demetrius and other Artemis salesmen declined. Sorcery was dwindling as well. Acts 19:19 says that those who had once been practicing such wickedness actually burned all of their books, the price of which is equivalent to approximately 50,000 days' wages. They didn't sell them and allow others to be led down the wrong path, they simply burned them. They lost money, but they did not seem to mind. It was all done for the cause of Christ! There were amazing things happening for the cause of Christ in the city of Ephesus even though the backdrop was horrific. Idolatry was spreading rapidly. Christians were hated by their neighbors and business associates because they dared go against the great goddess Artemis. The Roman government was breathing down their necks because they refused to worship any of the emperors. Growth was happening. Souls were being saved. But the societal climate around them? Wicked. Violent. Increasingly idolatrous. Hostile.

Paul's time in Ephesus was not easy. First, those in the synagogue rejected him. Next, both his life and his companions' lives were threatened by those whose pocketbooks were feeling the effects of Christianity's influence in the area. Yet Acts 19:10 shows that in such a time as that – with rejection and persecution abounding – the word of the Lord thrived. What does that say to us today? Do not be defeated when things seem to be going in a negative direction. God has always and will always use moments of what appear to be weakness to accomplish His greatest good. The question is, will you let Him?

Our world is consumed with its own form of idolatry; many today serve the idol of self. The world doesn't want to be told that they cannot watch certain things or listen to certain things or wear certain things. The world doesn't want to hear that there is only one way to heaven and that Jesus Christ is that way. The world doesn't want to have to give up their Sundays in order to worship or give up their alcohol for a sober and righteous lifestyle. Instead, the world wants to live like it wants to live: biting and devouring anyone who would threaten that way of life. Much like those in the angry mob in the theater at Ephesus, the world will raise their collective voice so that their chant acts as a bully against those who would be in opposition.

Think back to the acoustics in the Ephesian theater. If a mere whisper could be heard in the top rows, imagine what two hours of yelling must have sounded like. Those who were in support of Paul, and ultimately of Christ, must have been overwhelmed by the sheer volume of the impressive crowd.

We live in a world not unlike that of ancient Ephesus. With so many breathing threats against God's ways and those who would obey them, some Christians have been drawn away (or at the very least silenced) by the sinful, vocal majority. Like the believers in Ephesus, Christians today are bombarded on every side with people chanting and cheering for wickedness. Sometimes, we are tempted to give in – to slack off on God's commands in favor of the world's demands. Sometimes, the world's opposition to our way of life becomes more than we want to bear. Notice, though, that it becomes more than we *want* to bear, not more than we *can* bear. Those who had been dragged into the theater by an angry mob didn't renounce Christ or quit following Him even though they were threatened. Those who were previously involved in sorcery didn't hold onto their books just in case. Yet unlike those who gave up such wickedness in Ephesus, we are unwilling to give up sinful things that were important to us prior to our conversion and instead we act more like Demetrius, putting up a fuss when God's will encroaches on our bank account or lifestyle.

It is so sad that those in Ephesus would give their lives over to a false god; a statue that could do nothing for them. What is even more sad is that today, people reject the True and Living Son of God who literally came to earth and died on the cross for their sins. He did something! He gave up heaven and lived a life free of sin, only to be tortured, mocked, and crucified. Our God, the God, has shown up for us, and yet people reject Him. People who once claimed Him as their Lord reject Him. And for what? Stuff? So-called freedom? Hobbies? Ultimately, it is a temptation for us to serve the idol of self. We do what we think is in our best interest or what will bring us the most pleasure. Sometimes we call this worldliness.

First John 2:16 tells us what worldliness really is: giving in to the lust of the flesh, the lust of the eyes, and the pride of life. What do all of these things have in common? It's all about self. What my flesh craves. What my eyes want. How I can most enjoy life. Backing up one verse, John warns us that this kind of attitude means we do not have a true love for God. And how could we? If our focus is on self, how do we have room for anyone else? How are we loving God with our entire being (Mark 12:30) if we are putting our own desires above Him? Jesus said that if this is our attitude, we cannot be His disciples (Luke 14:26).

So how do we keep the world out? How do we keep ourselves from worshipping the idol of self, especially when we live in a society that seemingly demands we put ourselves first? Realize that it can be done. First Corinthians 10:13 is a very familiar verse that tells us that God is faithful to not allow us to be tempted above what we are able to bear, but will instead always give us a way to escape the temptation. What's less familiar is the verse immediately following, which says, "Therefore, my beloved, flee from idolatry."

Idolatry, even serving the idol of self, is something that can be overcome. It simply takes focus. And, of course, practice. Lots and lots of practice. Ultimately, though, it begins in our minds. God has created our minds to be such powerful tools, weapons really, that can be used in our fight against Satan. Satan, however, likes to take things that are good and use them for his own devices. Your mind is probably his most coveted possession. He wants it, yet God says guard it. So it's up to you to choose whose team you allow your mind to be used for and whose team you will allow it to be used against. Satan will try to captivate it with shiny things; things that attract your eyes

and your flesh, things that are self-serving, and things that will
lead you away from God. Don't let Satan deceive you. Instead,
"set your mind on things above, not on things on the earth"
(Col. 3:2). Fill your mind with things that are true, noble, just,
pure, and lovely (Phi. 4:8) and leave the rest behind.

In Romans 12:2, Paul says,

> And do not be conformed to this world, but be transformed by the
> renewing of your mind, that you may prove what is that good and
> acceptable and perfect will of God.

Here, Paul gives a contrast of the mind of a Christian
and the mind of someone living in idolatry. One who is self-
seeking is conformed to the world. They are drawn away by the
pleasures of the world, continually seeking to fulfill their own
desires above all and at any cost. They are fine doing things the
broad way, even though that will lead to destruction, as long
as it means happiness for now. Christians should not think
this way. The word translated "transformed" comes from the
Greek word *metamorphoō*, and even if you don't know Greek
you can see the similarity between that word and our English
word metamorphosis. Our minds are to completely change
form. Those in Ephesus who had once practiced sorcery had
such a change of mind that they burned their books! Their
minds experienced a complete overhaul. While they were once
self-serving, Christ changed that. When He entered their lives
(and minds), He caused them to think differently, and He'll do
the same for us. If we will choose to give ourselves to Him, He
will transform our minds from thinking too highly of ourselves
(Rom. 12:3) to placing the cause of Christ first and our own
desires last. When we've done that, there isn't really room for
the idol of self. Even though the world may be harassing us and
screaming at us and attempting to lure us to its sinful ways, we
can abstain because our minds are focused on Christ and His

will. We have undergone a complete metamorphosis. Despite the world's best efforts, He who is in us and He whose mind we have patterned ours after is "greater than he who is in the world" (1 John 4:4). Jesus is greater than any man-made idol and He is greater than we are, too. If we will simply align our mind with His, we will be able to overcome the world and the idol of self.

᪥

I. Have you ever faced persecution for doing things God's way? What were the circumstances? If you haven't, why do you think that's the case?

II. What would you consider to be idols in your own life?

III. When do you feel the most vulnerable to Satan's attacks?

IV. Think about the Greek word for "transformed" used in Romans 12:2. In what ways does your mind still need a metamorphosis?

V: What can you do this week to set your mind on Christ (Phi. 4:8; Col. 3:2)?

V

EXPOSING MATERIALISM
Ephesus

*Which do you love more:
riches or righteousness?*

༄~༄

Ephesus was by far the largest city in Anatolia, with approximately 300,000 inhabitants and thousands more continuously using the ever-important port, which was situated on the Aegean Sea in western Asia Minor. This port was the start of the Anatolian highway that ran through Laodicea and most of Asia Minor all the way to Syria. This allowed easy access for those taking the pilgrimage to the Artemisium, but also provided a large amount of commerce for the bustling city.

To accomodate the amount of industry and trade going on in Ephesus, there were two large marketplaces in the city. There would have been an exorbitant amount of trade going on in each agora, from food and clothing to statues of gods and goddesses. Trading was not the only function of the marketplace, however. The space would have also been used by popular philosophers and civic leaders for public speaking. These agoras would have been a buzzing, lively scene throughout the year! Surrounding the agoras would have been public baths, temples, and other large structures, making the area a one-stop shop for anything and everything a citizen needed to do.

Though most people would have done their shopping in the agora, it was not the only place in the city to conduct business. The grandiose Temple of Artemis, while mostly used as a worship facility, also functioned as a banking center and thus would have attracted a lot of business people as well.

There were other ways to spend money in Ephesus besides at the marketplace or Artemisium. Wealthy Ephesians could buy a terrace house, a very popular style of home in the first century. These houses were right in the city's center and boasted such features as indoor plumbing, mosaic (elaborately tiled) floors, and ornate frescos (paintings on the walls) that often depicted scenes from mythology. These usually multi-level houses were open, with columned courtyards and gardens in the center. Outside, marble streets go right from the doorstep down to the most bustling parts of the city. Clearly, these were elaborate dwellings!

For those whose wealth wasn't quite enough to be able to purchase a terrace house, money could also be spent at the nearby brothel. Ancient billboards have been uncovered in Ephesus, with symbols and directions carved right into the marble street that point toward the explicit complex. Seeing as the brothel was in the middle of the city, Ephesians did not appear embarrassed by their involvement in such immorality. On the contrary, such practices seemed to be embraced. Many were eager to spend their money in such an establishment.

Christians living in Ephesus were not only bombarded by idolatry on every corner, but were also surrounded by a people given over to greed and materialism. Sadly, they let these ideologies creep into their minds.

THE PASSAGE

The church in Ephesus received a letter from the Lord Himself by way of John's revelation. In Revelation 2:1-7, we read the

Lord's words to this struggling congregation:

> These things says He who holds the seven stars in His right hand, who walks in the midst of the seven golden lampstands: "I know your works, your labor, your patience, and that you cannot bear those who are evil. And you have tested those who say they are apostles and are not, and have found them liars; and you have persevered and have patience, and have labored for My name's sake and have not become weary.

It starts off pretty well, doesn't it? Jesus says that He knows their works, that they labor, are patient, and do not put up with those who are evil. They have combated false teaching and persevered in the face of adversity. These are amazing feats, especially in a city consumed by wickedness and idolatry. Verse four, however, shows a much bleaker picture:

> Nevertheless I have this against you, that you have left your first love. Remember therefore from where you have fallen; repent and do the first works, or else I will come to you quickly and remove your lampstand from its place--unless you repent. But this you have, that you hate the deeds of the Nicolaitans, which I also hate. He who has an ear, let him hear what the Spirit says to the churches. To him who overcomes I will give to eat from the tree of life, which is in the midst of the Paradise of God.

While the Ephesian Christians had done some things well, they had fallen short in the area that mattered most: their dedication to Christ. He was no longer the centerpiece of their lives, but instead had been taken off of the pedestal and replaced with, it seems, material possessions.

Timothy, who lived in Ephesus, received a letter from the apostle Paul that encouraged him to teach the people of Ephesus how they ought to conduct themselves. In 1 Timothy 6:7-10, Paul gave Timothy instruction on the problem of materialism:

> For we brought nothing into this world, and it is certain we can carry nothing out. And having food and clothing, with these we shall be content. But those who desire to be rich fall into temptation and a snare, and into many foolish and harmful lusts which drown men in destruction and perdition. For the love of money is a root of all kinds of evil, for which some have strayed from the faith in their greediness, and pierced themselves through with many sorrows.

Regrettably, many in Ephesus were absorbed by the desire to be rich instead of finding contentment in Christ (1 Tim. 6:6). This would prove to be both the downfall of individual Christians as well as the downfall of the Ephesian congregation as a whole. The pursuit of worldly gain seems to be what caused them to forsake their first love.

THE POINT

How do you leave your first love? We understand it from an earthly perspective, don't we? In a marriage, if each spouse does not continually choose to reach out to the other, to seek to better understand the other, and to lean on the other, the two will drift apart. If their interests become too different, they will drift. If something comes in and distracts one of them, they will start a gradual separation that, if left alone, will become too great to overcome. This is what happened to the church in Ephesus. These once strong, hardworking Christians had been distracted. Their interests changed. No longer were they chasing after God and His righteousness. Instead, they had become distracted from His service and consequently became involved with the world. They were committing spiritual adultery! How does that happen?!

While they had once been faithful Christians, materialism's hold was strong. In 1 Timothy 2:9-10, Timothy was instructed to tell the women of Ephesus how to dress in the worship assembly. Paul commanded Timothy to teach "that the women adorn themselves in modest apparel, with propriety and moderation, not with braided hair or gold or pearls or costly clothing, but, which is proper for women professing godliness, with good works."

The women in Ephesus were using their wealth (and their love of material things) as a means of distraction even in worship to God. They were showing up dressed elaborately, both in their clothing choices and their decorative hair arrangements. Paul told Timothy that this was not proper. A Christian's focus isn't to be on material things, but on spiritual treasures. Women who profess godliness shouldn't be flaunting wealth, but should instead be showing gentleness and meekness, propriety and moderation.

While this is just one passage relating specifically to women's choices of apparel, it's clear that this was a heart issue for many in Ephesus. Some of the wealthy men and women who had been converted to Jesus were having a hard time reprioritizing their lives. They absolutely wanted to worship God, but they also wanted to show off their money and how great they looked at the same time. They wanted the best of both worlds. They wanted to be in a relationship with God, but wanted to do a little "innocent flirting" with the world.

Don't let the Ephesian way of thinking fool you: when you decide to "flirt with" the world, you are cheating on God. Jesus says you cannot serve God and the world, because you'll either "hate the one and love the other, or else he will be loyal to the one and despise the other. You cannot serve God and mammon" (Mat. 6:24). James says that "friendship with the world is enmity with God" (4:4). There is no gray area here. Either you choose to be involved with the world or you choose God. Christ is either your life or He isn't, but there is no middle ground. You can't play the field with God. You are either in a monogamous relationship with Him or you are an adulterer. It's that simple.

For this reason, the church in Ephesus is urged to "remember therefore from where you have fallen; repent and do the first works" (Rev. 2:5). These Christians needed to go back to their first love, Christ. They needed to heed the words Paul wrote to Timothy in response to their materialistic mindset: "But you, O man of God, flee these things and pursue righteousness, godliness, faith, love, patience, gentleness. Fight the good fight of faith, lay hold on eternal life, to which you were also called and have confessed the good confession in the presence of many witnesses" (1 Tim. 6:11-12).

The word translated "pursue" is the same word that is often translated "persecution." The word literally means "to run swiftly in order to catch a person or thing, to pursue in a hostile manner." If we want to combat materialism, we must chase after righteousness. We cannot half-heartedly turn toward our Savior, as the Ephesians were trying to do. We must run for our lives – for our souls! With every part of who we are, we must pursue God. If we don't – if for some reason we choose to slack off – Satan's fiery darts of materialism and greed may very well hit us where it hurts.

If the Ephesian Christians teach us anything, it's that you can be striving to do good but still fall short. You can have good intentions, but have a heart that is in the wrong place. Sometimes we are tempted to pat ourselves on the back because we have given Jesus a place of prominence in our lives. The problem is, Jesus doesn't want a place of prominence in your life; He wants to be your life. If Jesus is merely a high priority, He's not a priority at all. To place anything in life anywhere remotely close to Him is an insult. After all, He is God. He is our Savior, who suffered and bled and died for our atonement and reconciliation. No, He doesn't simply occupy a place in our lives, He is our life. He is far above everything and everyone else, dwelling in an unapproachable light (1 Tim. 6:16).

Since we live in an age where we are blessed beyond measure with both physical and spiritual blessings, let Paul's closing words to Timothy be an exhortation to you:

> Command those who are rich in this present age not to be haughty, nor to trust in uncertain riches but in the living God, who gives us richly all things to enjoy. Let them do good, that they be rich in good works, ready to give, willing to share, storing up for themselves a good foundation for the time to come, that they may lay hold on eternal life (1 Tim. 6:17-19).

Having money isn't the issue, loving money is. If you have been blessed with material possessions, be sure you are using them to do good works. Do not store them up for yourself and do not place them above (or anywhere near!) your first love.

❧❦

I: What was the key problem facing the church in Ephesus (Rev. 2:4)?

II: How does one drift away from their first love?

III: In what ways has your zeal waned since your baptism?

IV: Are you tempted to let things get in the way of your dedication to Christ? Explain.

V: What two things does James call those who are 'just friends' with the world (James 4:4)?

VI

EXPOSING PERSECUTION
Pergamum

*Which do you fear more:
God or government?*

⤞⤝

Prior to the second century BC, there was no Roman governmental power in Asia Minor. All of that changed when Attalus III, king of Pergamum, died and left his kingdom to Rome in 133 BC, making Pergamum (sometimes written *Pergamos*) the first Roman province in all of Anatolia. Because of this extraordinary gift, the Roman government allowed Pergamum to build the first temple dedicated to the worship of the Roman emperor in 29 BC. Being home to an imperial cult, as it was known, was quite the honor, and would help Pergamum retain predominance in the region even after Ephesus rose to colossal power a few years later.

Just because the city housed a temple in which Roman emperors were worshiped didn't mean that every citizen was required to, that is, until 9 BC, when Fabius Maximus, proconsul (or governor) of Asia, issued a degree that stated that Emperor Augustus' birthday should be celebrated as a national holiday. This would have forced all those in Pergamum to worship Rome and the emperor. After all, "emperors made the same claims to deity as Jesus Christ, calling themselves lord, savior, creator, and god."[1] This requirement of imperial worship would have lasted throughout the first century (even after the church was established in the city) and into the second, when a massive and ornate temple to the Roman emperor Trajan was erected on the pinnacle of the city.

Having a temple to a Roman emperor on the highest point in the city of Pergamum was no small thing. First, the city's acropolis stands 1,300 feet above the valley below. Second, there were already numerous temples on the acropolis. There was the Temple of Athena, erected in the second century BC that had a 19-foot statue of the goddess inside. There was a temple to Dionysus, god of winemaking and religious ecstasy, situated at the base of the steepest theater in antiquity. And finally, there was an elaborate altar dedicated to Zeus. Yet above all of these, as a sort of subtle nod toward Rome's greatness and superiority, the imperial temple stood; towering above not only all of the residents below, but also high above the gods and goddesses that the city praised.

"Pliny the Elder called the city 'the most famous place of Asia,'"[2] though "most pagan" might have been a better description. In seemingly every way, the people of Pergamum were given over to fleshly lusts and false doctrines. They were proud of their status as hosting the first imperial cult in Asia and worked diligently to impress Rome any chance they had. They also prided themselves on being highly intelligent; Pergamum was home to the second largest library in antiquity, with 200,000 volumes filling the shelves. This impressive collection concerned those in Alexandria, Egypt (who boasted the largest library in the world), and so they stopped sending Pergamum papyrus, hoping that this would stop the creation

[1] Wilson, Mark W. *Biblical Turkey; A Guide to the Jewish and Christian Sites of Asia Minor.* Istanbul, Turkey: Ege Yayinlari, 2010. Print.
[2] *Ibid.*

of even more books. Not to be defeated, those in Pergamum invented (or at least, re-popularized) a new writing material known as pergamenum, or what we now call parchment (untanned animal skins). This export kept Pergamum a thriving city, but also in the good graces of Rome. Between the grandiose temples dedicated to emperors and the great resource that was parchment, Pergamum was an invaluable city to the Roman government, and one on which they would keep a close eye.

THE PASSAGE

While the city was mostly morally deficient, there was hope because there were Christians dwelling there. In Revelation 2:12-17, John records a letter written by Jesus to the church in Pergamum. As He always does, Jesus immediately declares that He "knows" the works of the church there, and for this congregation in particular, He seems to know their struggle.

> I know your works, and where you dwell, where Satan's throne is. And you hold fast to My name, and did not deny My faith even in the days in which Antipas was My faithful martyr, who was killed among you, where Satan dwells (v. 13).

Scholars are torn when it comes to the meaning of Satan's throne. Some would argue that the Altar of Zeus and the pagan practices that went on there would constitute this idea of Satan's throne, while others believe it is in reference to the imperial temple and the worship offered to Rome. Either way, the city was a hotbed of pagan immorality. It must have been incredibly difficult to live the holy life of a Christian in this city, and Jesus recognized their tribulation. Still, He didn't excuse their misdeeds.

But I have a few things against you, because you have there those who hold the doctrine of Balaam, who taught Balak to put a stumbling block before the children of Israel, to eat things sacrificed to idols, and to commit sexual immorality. Thus you also have those who hold the doctrine of the Nicolaitans, which thing I hate. Repent, or else I will come to you quickly and will fight against them with the sword of My mouth (v. 14-16).

While there was at least one faithful martyr in the city (Antipas, v. 13), many Christians were giving in to the sin that was running rampant around them. They were participating in the wickedness associated with idols in the city, likely so they could gain governmental favor and immunity. Such practices are sickening to our Lord, who says He has "the sharp two-edged sword" (v. 12) and will use it to fight should this letter not lead to repentance.

The use of the sword would have been a well-known thing for a Roman province. The Roman officials practiced *ius gladii,* or "right of the sword." This meant, in part, that any Roman officer had the right to condemn a man to death. You won't worship the emperor? Death. You won't proclaim Augustus as deity? Death. You have a problem with our altars and gods and goddesses? Death. In a city where pagan rituals were practiced on every corner and in every open space, it would have been tempting to give in if the alternative meant certain death. Yet Jesus speaks to His authority, an authority higher than Rome's, when urging these Christians to cling to Him and His way.

THE POINT

The letter to the church in Pergamum was meant to be an empowering one. While Rome might have lorded its authority over its citizens, Jesus Christ has all authority in heaven and on earth (Mat. 28:18). Rome might have exercised the right of the sword, but Jesus holds the two-edged sword. Such imagery brings to mind the description of the word of God that we read about in Hebrews 4:12-13:

> For the word of God is living and powerful, and sharper than any two-edged sword, piercing even to the division of soul and spirit, and of joints and marrow, and is a discerner of the thoughts and intents of the heart. And there is no creature hidden from His sight, but all things are naked and open to the eyes of Him to whom we must give account.

We shouldn't fear a government that can merely destroy our flesh. Instead, we should follow after the One who has the power to "destroy both soul and body in hell" (Mat. 10:28). Knowing this, though, and making it a reality in our lives are two different things. Being surrounded by thousands of people who dedicated their lives to one god or another and who saw no problem in bowing down to a mere man would have been difficult, especially if you were the only one not bowing down. Yet this is what our Lord has always and will always require.

Think about the book of Daniel. In Daniel 3 we read that King Nebuchadnezzar erected an image of gold and commanded all the people to bow down and worship it at a specified time. Shadrach, Meshach, and Abed-Nego refused, and they were brought before the king. Thinking that he could threaten them into submission, he gave them another chance to bow. When they refused for the second time, they were thrown into the blazing furnace.

While we know that God ultimately saved them and used the opportunity to bring Himself glory, Shadrach, Meshach, and Abed-Nego didn't know that was going to be the outcome. We know that from how they answer King Nebuchadnezzar's threats:

Our God whom we serve is able to deliver us from the burning fiery furnace, and He will deliver us from your hand, O king. But if not, let it be known to you, O king, that we do not serve your gods, nor will we worship the gold image which you have set up (Dan. 3:17-18).

In Pergamum, Christians faced certain death if they refused to bow down to the emperor of Rome. Knowing Antipas had already succumbed to such a brutal death made this an even more terrifying reality. It appears some were giving in to the pagan practices of their city in hopes of being spared such a fate, yet Jesus required the same of these Christians as He did the Christians in Smyrna: "Be faithful until death, and I will give you a crown of life" (Rev. 2:10).

This phrase doesn't simply mean be faithful until you've lived out your life on earth. The thrust of the phrase is actually be faithful *even if it means* death. In the face of certain death, be true to God. If you are given the choice between faithfulness or freedom from death, choose faithfulness.

Seeing that God required faithfulness in the face of death in both Old Testament and New Testament times, what do you think He demands in our modern time? While we may not live in a time when we are told to bow down to a man or image, we do live in an increasingly pagan society. More and more people claim "none" when it comes to religious affiliation, and an increasing amount of laws are being passed that give free rein to what God calls abominations. Sooner rather than later, the religious freedoms we've known in the past will be just that, a thing of the past. Preaching the gospel may become hate speech and prosecuted as such. The government may try to force you to do things God has said are wrong. But in every hypothetical scenario we can create, a Christian's response is the same: choose God over government.

As the beginning of the letter to Pergamum states, Jesus holds true authority. He had more authority than the Roman government and He has more power than our current governments. Men may attempt to pass laws that contradict God's law (like they did in implementing Augustus' birthday as a national holiday and subsequently making it a day to worship him), yet God's law is supreme. Men may make threats when we don't adhere to their godless laws, yet we must stand firm. Even if the entire world is bowing down, we stand, always honoring the true King and never fearing an earthly entity more than we fear Him.

Will it be easy to commit to this kind of life? Absolutely not. But now is the time to prepare ourselves. Now is the time to make the decision. As Joshua told the Israelites: choose this day whom you will serve. Make the choice right now that you will honor God in all of your actions for all of your days. Even when the government itself presses hard against you, you will remain faithful to God. Even when friends and family members give in to the unholy ways of the present culture, you will stay true to your Father. Even when your brothers and sisters in Jesus turn aside from His way in favor of governmental immunity, you will keep your eyes fixed on Jesus.

Our world makes it a habit to overstep its bounds. It demands our loyalty and respect and honor all the while going against God's laws. Do not give in to the temptation to bend to the government's will. Instead, submit to God. Follow after His will and His will alone. Do nothing that would align you with the world, but rather seek His way in your every decision.

Let this prayer be ever on our lips: "Direct my steps by Your word, and let no iniquity have dominion over me" (Psa. 119:133).

꙳⸱꙳

I: Why were Shadrach, Meshach, and Abed-Nego thrown into the fiery furnace?

II: Write out their response to King Nebuchadnezzar (Dan. 3:17-18).

III: In what ways is your government seeking to take away religious liberties?

IV: Read Joshua 24:14-15. Will you make the same declaration Joshua makes at the end of verse 15, even if government oppression comes? Choose today.

V: Write Psalm 119:133 on a sticky note. Place it somewhere you will see it frequently.

VII

EXPOSING RATIONALIZATION
Thyatira

Do you have any pet sins in your life?

❧

The city of Thyatira was settled in 281 BC as a Grecian military colony, but experienced numerous sieges because of its expansive, defenseless location on the plains of central Asia Minor. The Roman Empire would overtake the city, as well as the majority of Asia Minor, and would bring increased prosperity to the region. Thyatira was said to be one of the largest inland cities in the New Testament era. In ancient times, most of the large towns were situated on or near a port, yet a landlocked Thyatira was still a thriving city. It was the midway point between the larger cities of Sardis and Pergamum, and the highway running directly through the city center connected to two other significant cities, Smyrna and Bithynia. Because of this ideal location, Thyatira became a city of trade, establishing itself as one of the largest commercial centers of the region.

One of the city's most prosperous exports was wool that was dyed a specific color of purple. Those in Thyatira would use the madder root, native to that region, to make the highly sought after purple dye. It is no wonder, then, that the first introduction we have to this city in the New Testament is when we meet a woman named Lydia, who was by trade a seller of purple (Acts 16:14).

Thanks to the notoriety that the purple dye industry brought, archeological evidence suggests that the city had three gymnasiums and quite a few temples. Due to the fact that so many stopped off the busy highway to buy, sell, and trade in the city, many merchants set up shop in Thyatira. Not surprisingly, "inscriptional evidence indicates that the city was host to numerous trade guilds, which functioned as social, civic, and religious clubs or organizations."[1] These guilds would have included merchants who were potters, wool-workers, shoe makers, and, most notably, purple dyers.

Part of the popularity of the trade guilds was likely due in part to the festivities surrounding such guilds. These clubs, each of which had a patron god or goddess, held elaborate banquets in pagan temples, and "after eating, the diners often engaged in sexually immoral acts on the couches where they reclined."[2] Clearly, these guilds were as much for social enjoyment and sexual pleasure as they were for the benefit of one's trade.

THE PASSAGE

The church in Thyatira is the fourth of the seven churches of Asia listed in the book of Revelation, and in their letter from the Lord they received both praise and a stern warning. Theirs is actually the longest of the letters, in which Jesus detailed the good that they were doing as well as the areas that needed

---

[1] Fant, Clyde E., and Mitchell Glenn Reddish. *A Guide to Biblical Sites in Greece and Turkey*. New York: Oxford UP, 2003. Print. 328.

[2] Wilson, Mark W. *Biblical Turkey; A Guide to the Jewish and Christian Sites of Asia Minor*. Istanbul, Turkey: Ege Yayinlari, 2010. Print.

special, immediate attention. Here is a portion of Jesus' words to the struggling congregation:

> I know your works, love, service, faith, and your patience; and as for your works, the last are more than the first. Nevertheless I have a few things against you, because you allow that woman Jezebel, who calls herself a prophetess, to teach and seduce My servants to commit sexual immorality and eat things sacrificed to idols. And I gave her time to repent of her sexual immorality, and she did not repent. Indeed I will cast her into a sickbed, and those who commit adultery with her into great tribulation, unless they repent of their deeds. I will kill her children with death, and all the churches shall know that I am He who searches the minds and hearts. And I will give to each one of you according to your works (Rev. 2:19-23).

The church in the bustling city of Thyatira had a few things going for them. They were a working people whose faith, service, and love were all commended by the Lord. Still, they were not without issues. Their problem was that a few Christians were still involved in pagan practices. Likely, it was those within the trade guilds who were hanging on to the immoral rituals associated with such.

The reference to Jezebel, then, makes perfect sense, because in the Old Testament, Jezebel was the woman who brought idol worship to the Israelites through her marriage to King Ahab (1 Kings 16:31-33). Consequently, she was the one to lead the Israelites down the path of unfaithfulness to God. In the same way, those in Thyatira were being led away from righteousness and into infidelity; participating in pagan practices that, to God, were the equivalent to spiritual adultery. Specifically, these people were involved in sexual immorality and eating things sacrificed to idols, both of which would have been common practice at the feasts put on by the trade guilds. Therefore, it seems that the heart of the issue in Thyatira was that there were those holding tightly to their professional commitments instead of giving their allegiance to Christ.

Jesus went on to say that practicing such abominations was to "know the depths of Satan" (Rev. 2:24). While there were some willing to do good, others were willing to forsake their Lord simply to keep their professional ties intact. Such people were not only severing their personal relationship with Jesus, but were also sinking the church in Thyatira.

THE POINT

While today we are not necessarily involved in trade guilds, worldly pleasures do still draw us away from our Lord. When we are enticed by what Satan places before our eyes and hearts, we rationalize why those sins are acceptable. We tell ourselves that participating in a certain sin is fine so long as it is for work or a relationship or some other seemingly good reason. We excuse our immorality because it helps us get ahead in one way or another. In this way, it seems we behave much like those in Thyatira.

What do you place above your relationship with Christ? You may think, *"Nothing."* However, if you are willing to excuse any sin, you are saying that such an activity or attitude is more important to you than Jesus. If someone goes to the office Christmas party and consumes alcohol for the sake of blending in with their colleagues, they are saying that such things are more important to them than their Savior. If someone is unwilling to get out of an adulterous relationship or stop committing fornication, they are saying that a person, or simply sexual pleasure, is more important to them than Jesus. If someone allows participating in a golf tournament or other sporting event to take precedence over worshiping God, they are saying that those things are of more value than He is.

Seem extreme? In Matthew 10:37-38, Jesus said,

He who loves father or mother more than Me is not worthy of Me.
And he who loves son or daughter more than Me is not worthy
of Me. And he who does not take his cross and follow after Me is
not worthy of Me.

If we put anyone above Jesus, even our parents or spouse or children, we are not worthy to be called His disciple. If we cannot even put relationships that are wholesome above our relationship with Christ, what could possibly make us rationalize that putting sin above Him is acceptable?

In Matthew 19, we read the account of a young man coming to Jesus with the intent of learning more about eternal life. He asks Jesus what he must do in order to inherit it, and Jesus tells him to keep the commandments. Excitedly, the young man tells Jesus that he has kept all of the commands of God from his youth. With that, Jesus says to him, "If you want to be perfect, go, sell what you have and give to the poor, and you will have treasure in heaven; and come, follow Me" (Mat. 19:21). What happened next is what happens to so many people in today's world, and what was happening to so many in Thyatira. The young man went away from Jesus sorrowful, because he wasn't willing to put Jesus above his own desires. In his case, he had a lot of possessions and he didn't want to part with them.

In Thyatira, there were Christians who had a major involvement in trade guilds and they were unwilling to give them up, likely because it would mean a decrease in business and wealth. Because they held on so tightly to their guild memberships, they loosened the grip they had on Jesus. In today's world we do the same thing. We find something we really enjoy, a "pet sin" some call it, and we are unwilling to let it go. We do everything we can to justify our participation in such things, when the reality is simple: you cannot love anything more than you love God. There is no getting around that. No amount of rationalization will make it acceptable. Either God is everything to you or He is nothing. Either you are willing to forsake all and follow Him, or you are not worthy to be called His disciple. While we want to blur the lines and make gray areas, God has made His will abundantly clear. He wants all of us; He wants to possess every part of our heart.

Notice that in the letter Jesus wrote to the Christians in Thyatira He said He is the one who "searches the minds and hearts" (Rev. 2:23). It is not merely enough to do all of the right things or for those around you to see you doing all the right things. God looks at the heart. If in our hearts we are placing wealth, popularity, sexual pleasure, entertainment, relationships, or anything else above Him, He knows. He sees the priorities of our hearts. He knows how our minds rationalize our actions. We cannot fool God! If He is not above all, He is nothing. We may not think that; no, we may justify ourselves and rationalize why that's not the case. Ultimately, though, that is how God views it. We are either for Him or against Him. We are either in a committed relationship with Him or we are His enemy.

Those in Thyatira believed they were righteous. Many of them were likely involved in the good works that Jesus mentioned at the beginning of His letter to them. Sadly, they had fooled themselves into thinking that they could have one hand on God and the other hand clinging to all of the things they had enjoyed in their past life. Christian, know that Satan will use this tactic on you as well. He will attempt to deceive you into thinking that you can still be a disciple and be involved in things God calls abominable. Don't be fooled! Where there is iniquity, there is no God. If you choose to be involved in sin, God is not abiding in you. Light and darkness cannot exist together.

Dig deep into the recesses of your heart and think about the things that are most important to you. Ask yourself if you are holding on to something that you know is sinful. While it may be difficult to let go, realize that no matter how much you try to justify it, participating in sin is always wrong. Entertaining even the smallest amount of iniquity in your life is separating you from your God.

God wants His people to be clean. He wants His people to be free from sin and wholly His. When we rationalize our sin and keep it close to us, we are distancing ourselves from God. Don't do that! God wants to be close to you. He wants to call you His. That is why He sent His Son to die. So you could abandon the life of sin that was leading you to death and follow after the One who will show you the way to life. But know this: you cannot walk toward life everlasting if you are unwilling to let go of sin. So let go! Let go of whatever pet sin you're holding on to and justifying in your mind. It is not worth losing your soul!

꘎꘎

I: Why do you think the Christians in Thyatira struggled with sexual immorality and food sacrificed to idols?

II: What types of sins are Christians tempted to rationalize in our modern world?

III: Do you have things in your life that you know are wrong but you hang onto anyway? List scriptures that would condemn such activities or attitudes.

IV: What types of things act as Jezebels in our present world and lure people away from God?

V: Do you think people saying "God wants me to be happy" is an example of rationalizing sin? Why or why not?

VIII

EXPOSING COMPLACENCY
Laodicea

Do you feel good enough just the way you are?

৵∘৽

Laodicea is located in the earthquake-prone region of Phrygia in central Asia Minor. Though established in 260 BC, the city would not flourish until many years later. In 27 AD, though beginning to rise economically, the city literally fell due to an earthquake and relied on Rome to help them with the rebuilding process. Shortly thereafter, in 60 AD, the city was at its peak; so much so, when another major earthquake struck the region that very year, Laodicea was the only city to reject Roman help as they restructured.

Perhaps the wealth of the city was due in part to its highly desirable location. Positioned on the Anatolian Highway (a highway that ran from Ephesus all the way across modern-day Turkey), Laodicea became a critical part of the trade route between Jerusalem and Ephesus. One such item that would have been used in trade came directly from Laodicea: a black wool that the Romans used for making tunics and cloaks. Because of the great amount of trade (of both its own resources and those passing through on the highway), Laodicea established itself as a banking city that would ultimately go on to mint its own coins.

With wealthy cities come a host of different structures. Grandiose temples, multiple theaters, an agora, and impressive baths lined the city streets, as did a medical school that specialized in ophthalmology. The eye became a focus of doctors in the city because massive amounts of zinc were produced in Laodicea and the surrounding areas, and it was a critical ingredient in a famous eye salve (known as Phrygian powder) that was linked to the city.

Another note of interest is that Laodicea had some very close neighboring cities. Known as the Tri-Cities of the Lycus River, Laodicea, Hierapolis, and Colossae were often linked together. Colossae was approximately 10 miles east of Laodicea, while Hierapolis was a mere six miles north. Though they were close in proximity, the cities themselves (and their geography!) could not have been more different.

While Laodicea had the distinction of being the wealthiest city, Colossae had once been an impressive place as well. Nestled just below the snow-capped Mount Cadmus, it was established long before the other two cities, yet began losing some of its luster when Laodicea was chosen as the route for the bustling highway.

Hierapolis, on the other hand, had attractions of its own that kept the city in a favorable position even after Laodicea rose in prestige. The city, known today as Pamukkale, has countless hot springs that lose carbon dioxide and leave limestone deposits (known as white calcium carbonate) along the mountainside. Though Colossae is technically the city that sits at the base of snow-capped mountains, Hierapolis is the one that looks snowy! Venture close enough to see the steam and feel the warmth of the waters and you will know, however, that you couldn't be more wrong.

Many in the first century time period viewed the hot springs of Hierapolis as magical; possessing healing powers that could cure a host of ailments and diseases. People flocked from all over for the warmth and relief that this ancient city provided.

Though Laodicea was far less touristy than Hierapolis, it still boasted unmatched wealth, scholarship, and resources for that region of Asia Minor. Sadly, this would be the downfall of the city.

THE PASSAGE

Laodicea is among the seven churches of Asia Minor listed in Revelation 1-3, though their account is a troubling one. When you read Revelation 3:14-22, you are faced with an unsavory truth: these Christians were not patterning their lives after Christ. Instead, they had become a people of complacency, assuming that because of their city's grand accolades they were somehow right with God. This could not have been less true.

Jesus told them,

> I know your works, that you are neither cold nor hot. I could wish you were cold or hot. So then, because you are lukewarm, and neither cold nor hot, I will vomit you out of My mouth (Rev. 3:15-16).

It is interesting that this is the picture Jesus gives to describe their mediocrity, because the Laodiceans would have been very familiar with the concept of being neither hot nor cold.

Think back to the geographical location of the city. Six miles north, a city known for its hot springs. 10 miles east, a city resting below the beauty and splendor of snow-capped mountains and beside cold mountain streams. Laodicea, right in the center, was neither hot nor cold. Instead, they were lukewarm, and their spiritual state had come to match their geography perfectly.

Jesus does not simply know the geographical location of these people; He knows everything about both their city and their heart. In verse 17, Jesus has the Laodiceans saying, "I am rich, have become wealthy, and have need of nothing!" Is this not exactly how the Laodiceans responded to the Roman government after the 60 AD earthquake? They were the only city to refuse help because they wanted everyone to know how wealthy and self-sufficient they were! This mindset, this city pride, had even crept into the church and was destroying their souls. Jesus sternly reprimanded them and told them that they were not wealthy nor self-sufficient, but instead were "wretched, miserable, poor, blind, and naked."

These words would have cut the Laodiceans to the heart. Poor? We mint our own coins! Blind? We created a famous eye salve! Naked? Even Rome wants our wool to create tunics! Yet none of these things amount to anything in the eyes of Jesus. Wealth means nothing. Riches do not buy salvation. Medicine is not a balm for your soul. Fancy clothes cannot cover up an ugly heart. The Laodiceans thought they were something, but Jesus showed them that without Him, they were nothing. They were wretched and miserable. And without Him, we are, too.

THE POINT

When we self praise, as these Laodiceans did, Jesus finds no praise. When we make our lives all about us, it puts us in a place of complacency; standing still instead of pressing toward the prize (Phi. 3:12-14). The terrible and terrifying thing about that type of attitude is that Jesus says it makes Him sick! Revelation 3:16 says Jesus will "vomit" these lukewarm Christians out of His mouth! What graphic imagery, and yet what sobering thoughts. Should you and I become mediocre in our Christian walk, we would be making our Lord and Savior sick. This thought should shake us to our very core. It should move us out of neutral and into overdrive. It should make us reassess everything! We should ask ourselves if we are in control and leading our lives in the right direction or if Christ is in control and leading our lives in a heavenward direction.

Ultimately, self-reliance makes us poor. When we think we have arrived and attained as much as we need, we are really admitting that we are depleted; utterly destitute and void of righteousness.

In Mark 8:34-37, Jesus says,

> Whoever desires to come after Me, let him deny himself, and take up his cross, and follow Me. For whoever desires to save his life will lose it, but whoever loses his life for My sake and the gospel's will save it. For what will it profit a man if he gains the whole world, and loses his own soul? Or what will a man give in exchange for his soul?

To truly be disciples of Jesus, we must be willing to deny ourselves. That denial involves denying that we have achieved anything good on our own. It is only by God's grace that we have salvation. Anything else we have achieved, Paul would call "loss" for the cause of Christ (Phi. 3:7). Nothing besides salvation matters, and in no way have we earned any part of that. And so, we deny ourselves. We deny that anything we've accomplished has been by our own doing, and we deny any other selfishness that might try to creep in and tempt us with an attitude of self-reliance or complacency.

Notice that Jesus continued by saying that those whose chief desire is worldly possessions and profit are those who are going to be lost for eternity. You cannot set your affections on earth and then have heaven as your final destination. That would make heaven an afterthought, and it is in no way an afterthought! It is the place that Jesus Christ has gone to prepare for us. It is the place God wants us to be so badly that, in order to make a way for us to access it, He gave His own Son to die on the cross. Shame on us if we choose, then, to dwell on earthly things and temporary things instead of dwelling on the sacrifice of Jesus and the inheritance that God has promised. Shame on us if we let our spirituality stall or take a backseat to the things we want to do or store up for ourselves.

Perhaps you don't struggle with focusing on worldly things instead of Jesus, but you may still fall into the trap of the Laodiceans. You see, these people were content, but not in a Biblical way. They thought they had done enough. They thought they were good enough – that their reputation was enough to sit back and rest on. Sure, they likely weren't the best people in the world, but they weren't the worst. They didn't do horrendously terrible things, though they didn't do many great things either. Jesus says that this doesn't cut it. You are not a faithful Christian if you are a lukewarm Christian. Instead, you must "be zealous and repent" (Rev. 3:19).

The Hebrews writer issues one of the sternest warnings in all of Scripture in Hebrews 6:4-6. He says,

> For it is impossible for those who were once enlightened, and have tasted the heavenly gift, and have become partakers of the Holy Spirit, and have tasted the good word of God and the powers of the age to come, if they fall away, to renew them again to repentance, since they crucify again for themselves the Son of God, and put Him to an open shame.

Often, we associate this passage with backsliding into sin. While it is most definitely applicable in that regard, the passage itself isn't speaking to that in the original context. If you back up to Hebrews 5:12-14, you see that these people were not growing. They had been Christians for long enough that they should have been teachers, but instead, they were still on a milk diet instead of solid food. Hebrews 6 opens in this context. The writer urges these Jewish Christians to move forward, because standing still is moving backward (v. 4-6).

These were people who had a form of zeal. They were good at helping others (Heb. 6:10-12), but they were stalled when it came to spiritual growth. They weren't moving forward. And so Jesus' words to the Laodiceans in Revelation 3 ring out in our minds. If you are neither hot nor cold, you make Him sick. Failing to move forward is moving backward. This is a theme throughout the entire New Testament!

Don't let yourself fall into the complacent trap. Don't ever assume you know enough about any particular Scripture or concept in the Bible. Don't let yourself think that doing one good thing (like helping others) excuses you from keeping the other commandments of God. That's how you become complacent. That's how you get comfortable. Being a disciple of the Lord isn't about comfort, it's about continually being molded into the image of Christ. None of us would ever claim to be on the same level of Jesus, and yet He's our standard. That means there is always room for improvement and never room for sitting back and taking it easy. After all, this is a race. Let's run it with endurance, "ever looking to Jesus as the author and finisher of our faith" (Heb. 12:1-2).

≈∘≈

I: What contrast is Jesus giving when He speaks of the following conditions of the Laodiceans in Revelation 3:17-18:
   - Poor (v. 17): _____
   - Blind (v. 17): _____
   - Naked (v. 17): _____
   - White garments (v. 18): _____

II: In what ways do you think the present world is like Laodicea?

III: What can you do to keep yourself from becoming complacent?

IV: List one area you think you excel in and one area you think you neglect in your spiritual journey.

V: List the accomplishments Paul counts as loss for Christ in Philippians 3:4-7.

IX

EXPOSING VULNERABILITY
Sardis

Does Satan have a foothold in your heart?

❧

Situated roughly 60 miles inland from the booming port city of Ephesus and resting on the banks of the Pactolus River, Sardis was an important city in Asia Minor throughout history. Settled around 1400 BC, it was once the capital city of the Lydian empire. This longstanding city saw it all: epic battles, mighty empires, and conquering kings. There was even a large Jewish population thanks to the protection administered by Queen Esther of Persia (Est. 7:1-4).

The city, due to its enduring presence, has had many rich stories in its history. Perhaps the most notorious is that of the fall of the king of Lydia, King Croesus. Croesus ruled from 560-547 BC and generated unmatched wealth for Sardis. He is said to have even helped fund the construction of the great Temple of Artemis in Ephesus. Sadly, for all the wealth, respect, and attention he garnered for Sardis, his story did not end well.

Sardis, like most cities of antiquity, had an upper city and lower city. The upper city of Sardis sat on the acropolis, a fortified area that was said to be impregnable. This is where King Croesus's palace was, and where most of the military might of the city was stationed. No one could penetrate this great acropolis, and Sardis won many battles against those who dared try. Not surprisingly, King Croesus became a bit arrogant, and when he heard that the Persians were gaining strength nearby, he attacked them. The battle ended in a draw, and the Lydian king retreated back to his seemingly indestructible acropolis. The Persians, however, followed, hoping to find a susceptible area to attack.

The tradition is that not many days after settling back in, one of the Lydian guards stationed on the acropolis dropped his helmet. Instead of going the long way down to retrieve it, he took a secret passage that exposed an extreme military vulnerability to the hidden Persian army. Waiting until just the right moment, the Persians pounced and overtook what most assumed was an impenetrable area! Thus, "the acropolis was taken through a security lapse"[1] and the rest is history. Sardis was conquered by the Persians.

While command of the city would change hands, it would not be the end for Sardis. Instead, the city saw steady growth. In 334 BC construction began on a massive temple to Artemis, the ruins of which are the best preserved of any Artemisium in Asia Minor. Sardis kept growing for centuries after that, too, as is evidenced by the construction of an enormous gymnasium/ bath house in the early second century. The ruins for these structures are impressive even today, so one can only imagine the grandeur of the city of Sardis in its prime.

THE PASSAGE

Intellectually, we understand that God knows everything, yet sometimes we fail to dwell on that fact. While reading through the letters to the seven churches of Asia, it is easy

[1] Wilson, Mark W. *Biblical Turkey; A Guide to the Jewish and Christian Sites of Asia Minor.* Istanbul, Turkey: Ege Yayinlari, 2010. Print.

to read "I know your works" but another thing altogether to fully appreciate the reality of Jesus' words. The letter written to the church in Sardis gives us one of those "aha!" moments. Here, Jesus seems to play off the city's well-known (though somewhat embarrassing) history and uses it to show what is lacking in the congregation.

> These things says He who has the seven Spirits of God and the seven stars: "I know your works, that you have a name that you are alive, but you are dead. Be watchful, and strengthen the things which remain, that are ready to die, for I have not found your works perfect before God. Remember therefore how you have received and heard; hold fast and repent. Therefore if you will not watch, I will come upon you as a thief, and you will not know what hour I will come upon you. You have a few names even in Sardis who have not defiled their garments; and they shall walk with Me in white, for they are worthy. He who overcomes shall be clothed in white garments, and I will not blot out his name from the Book of Life; but I will confess his name before My Father and before His angels. He who has an ear, let him hear what the Spirit says to the churches."

Reread the letter and think about the imagery of the thief that Jesus gives. Notice especially the words "watchful", "watch", and "come upon you." Was this not exactly what had happened to the city of Sardis under the reign of King Croesus? Had they not neglected to be watchful? Did not their lack of diligence lead to their downfall? It seems the same thing was happening to the Christians in the first century. They were failing to be watchful. They were exposing their weaknesses to the enemy. Fortunately for them, it was not too late. Jesus was showing them their own vulnerability and giving them the chance to repent.

These Christians had a reputation for being good, for being alive, and yet their reality was spiritual death. They had left themselves wide open to the enemy; their defenses were down while they rested on their laurels because of past faithfulness. Jesus told them that this was a deadly serious problem, and Christians today will do well to heed the same warning.

THE POINT

The enemy that the church in Sardis had left themselves exposed to is the same enemy that we face today. Just as the Persian army was waiting outside the walls of the city for a moment of weakness, so too is our enemy, Satan. First Peter 5:8 instructs us to "be sober, be vigilant, because your adversary the devil walks about like a roaring lion, seeking whom he may devour."

The word that is translated "vigilant" is the same word that is translated in our text from Revelation 3 as "watch," though the meaning is much deeper than our English texts suggest. The word does not simply mean to be awake, but rather to be wide awake; aroused from slumber and on high alert. Reading through the remainder of 1 Peter 5:8 gives us the reasoning behind such watchfulness: Satan is lying in wait seeking to utterly consume us. He is walking around the walls of our hearts, waiting for us to leave a place unguarded so that he can come inside and wreak havoc. Knowing this, what do we do about it? Do we continue in our spiritual slumber or do we put ourselves on high alert? The Christians in Sardis had unfortunately gone to sleep, but if we do not want to receive the same condemnation that they did, we will choose to remain alert.

In 1 Corinthians 10, Paul reaches back to the Old Testament example of the children of Israel to show what types of things the Corinthians should not be involved in. He lists things such as idolatry, sexual immorality, and complaining, then concludes the discussion in this way: "Therefore let him who thinks he stands take heed lest he fall" (v. 12).

It is tempting to read through Scripture and assume none of those terrible things could ever happen to us. We would never leave our first love. We would never let Satan creep into our hearts. We would never (insert sin here). Be careful with that thinking. Paul says to "take heed" or, better translated, "weigh carefully." Is it really so inconceivable that you might fall? Moses, a friend of God, did; striking the rock when God said to speak to it. David, a man after God's own heart, did; committing adultery with Bathsheba. Peter, who walked with our Lord, did; denying Him three times before the crucifixion. Is it really impossible to think we could leave our hearts exposed? Jesus says it is very possible, which is why we must stand ready, sober and vigilant at all times.

Satan's ultimate objective is to find you vulnerable and exposed when the Lord returns. He wants to distract you from service; to keep your eyes and heart locked on the world so that you are not ready when Jesus comes again. For that reason, Jesus gave special attention to the Judgment and being ready for that day to come.

In Mark 13:32-36, Jesus says,

But of that day and hour no one knows, not even the angels in heaven, nor the Son, but only the Father. Take heed, watch and pray; for you do not know when the time is. It is like a man going to a far country, who left his house and gave authority to his servants, and to each his work, and commanded the doorkeeper to watch. Watch therefore, for you do not know when the master of the house is coming – in the evening, at midnight, at the crowing of the rooster, or in the morning – lest, coming suddenly, he find you sleeping. And what I say to you, I say to all: Watch!

Jesus does not want us to be unprepared to meet Him. His entire purpose in coming to earth was to seek and save the lost (Luke 19:10). He does not want even one of His sheep to be astray when He comes, and so He encourages us all to watch! We do not know when we will die, nor do we know when Jesus will come to claim His own. We do know, however, that we have right now – this very moment – to do His will. To stand watching, guarding our hearts and minds from Satan, continually involved in good works and faithful service to our Father.

Satan wants you to forget about the Judgment Day. Satan wants you to feel indestructible, because that is when you are the most vulnerable to his advances. Don't let his tactics deceive you. The Judgment of God is very real. Jesus will come as a thief in the night. If you are not living in a sober state, now is the time. Do as Jesus instructed the church in Sardis and "be watchful," "hold fast," "strengthen the things which remain," and "repent!" As the familiar hymn goes, "leave no unguarded place, no weakness of the soul."[2]

In order to be on the lookout for Satan's advances, you must first recognize that it can happen to *you*. *You* can fall away. *You* can be lead down the wrong path. Realize that Satan is a very real and present threat, then do all within your power to keep him at bay. Pray without ceasing, as this will guard your heart and mind in Christ (Phi. 4:6-7). Have a forgiving spirit, lest Satan enter your heart through bitterness (2 Cor. 2:10-11). Dig deeply into the Scriptures, so you will not find yourself in opposition to them (2 Tim. 2:15, 25-26). When we know God's word, apply it to our hearts, and pray for strength and the ability to forgive liberally, our defenses are made strong. Our vulnerabilities will become fewer and fewer. Just know that

---

[1] Wesley, Charles. *Soldiers of Christ, Arise.* 1749.

now is the time to take these precautions. Now is the time to fortify the walls of your heart. If you wait until Satan throws a fiery dart, it may be too late.

Just as Jesus knew the works and heart of the church in Sardis, Jesus knows you. He sees your heart. He sees your vulnerabilities. He sees the areas you have left exposed to Satan, and throughout the New Testament, the Holy Spirit gives us the same warnings that Jesus gave those in Sardis. Watch out! Be sober! Guard your heart and mind! If you don't, the consequences will be deadly. However, if you will heed the Scriptures, you can rest assured that you will be victorious. James promises us that if we resist the devil's advances, "he will flee from you" (James 4:7).

While Satan is an enemy crouching at the door of our hearts, he only has as much power as we give him. In reality, his power is laughable compared to the One who rules our lives. Therefore, when God's people resist, he retreats. He does not want to go up against Almighty God! Be sure, then, that you are actively seeking to defend your heart. Remain on guard, watching for and deflecting Satan's advances. When you do, he will flee. But remember, if at any point you let your guard down, he will be back, aiming his darts in your direction. So never give up. Never fall asleep. Be watchful and vigilant, and God will give you strength.

I: Who is our enemy and what is he pictured as in 1 Peter 5:8?

II: What vulnerabilities does Satan use to get into your heart?

III: What ways can you combat these tactics?

IV: In what ways do you find yourself spiritually asleep? Lack of study or prayer? Lack of good works? Make a list and pray about them this week.

V: List ways you can "be sober and vigilant" in the coming weeks to thwart Satan's advances.

X

EXPOSING DISCOURAGEMENT
Crete

*Does the wickedness around you
paralyze or propel you?*

Crete is both the southernmost and largest of the Greek islands, and also one of the earliest to be inhabited. Its history is expansive, as it was founded around 3000 BC and is considered the birthplace for the ancient peoples known as the Philistines. Much like other regions in Greece and Asia Minor, Crete was conquered by many different armies, the final being the Roman empire around 67 BC.

After being established as a Roman colony, Crete was turned into your typical Greco-Roman place: theaters, baths, imperial temples, and amphitheaters were all constructed on the 150-mile long island. Since Crete is very mountainous (its mountain range spanning roughly the entire length of the island,) most of these buildings were located on the northern part of the island, for the southern part was far too sloped to be inhabitable. While southern Crete did not boast immaculate cities, it was renowned for its natural harbors. One such harbor, Fair Havens, is mentioned in Acts 27:8 as Luke recounts Paul's tumultuous journey.

In the early sixth century BC, a poet named Epimenides lived on the island and wrote about the general character of the Cretan people. Quoted by Paul in his letter to Titus, the

Cretans were called, "liars, evil beasts, and lazy gluttons" (Titus 1:12). Epimenides would not be the only writer to give such disparaging comments about Crete; many writers of old associated the people of Crete with having nearly nonexistent ethical principles, being involved in pirating and other means of dishonest gain, and being greedy. It's unfortunate that this description was confirmed as true in reference to the Cretans of first century times as well (Titus 1:13).

Fortunately, there was hope for this morally deficient city, and that hope was Jesus Christ. We know from Acts 2 that Cretans were among those present on the day of Pentecost, and as a result it is likely some were converted and took the message of the gospel back to Crete. By the time Paul left Titus on the island (approximately 63-65 AD), there were multiple congregations (Titus 1:5). Titus was instructed to establish elders and to strengthen the Christians who were failing to live up to the new standard to which they had been called.

THE PASSAGE

It must have been difficult for Titus, a relatively young preacher who had been left on a far away island, to minister in a place full of lazy, evil, and gluttonous people. Still, he had a job to do: to "set in order the things that are lacking" and "speak the things which are proper for sound doctrine" (Titus 1:5, 2:1). Paul's instructions for how to do so came in the form of urging the people toward good works. If the people would "deny ungodliness and worldly lusts" (2:12), they would be fit to wear the name of Christ.

It was going to take effort, though, because there were "many insubordinate, idle talkers and deceivers" who needed to be rebuked (1:10, 13). Still, it could be done, and Titus was there to tell them how to do it.

Paul encouraged Titus to exhort the young men to "be a pattern of good works" (Titus 2:7). In 3:1, he was commanded to tell the entire congregation to "be ready for every good work." But what do good works have to do with it? Why was this so crucial for the Cretans to know? How would this help their lying, evil, gluttonous society?

From Ephesians 2:10 we know that doing good works is our purpose as Christians. But why? In Matthew 5:16, Jesus said we are to let our lights shine to the world around us so that those good works can bring glory to God. Peter said the same thing in 1 Peter 2:12:

> Having your conduct honorable among the Gentiles, that when they speak against you as evildoers, they may, by your good works which they observe, glorify God in the day of visitation.

The Cretan Christians were not encouraged to parade their good works in front of people for the sake of being seen and given a pat on the back; instead, they were commanded to be a people who "maintain good works" (Titus 3:14) because this brings honor to God. When people see Christians doing good, they are ultimately seeing the goodness of God extended, and they will glorify Him for His grace and mercy.

The Christians living on Crete would have once been just like all of the other Cretans. Titus 3:3 says:

> For we ourselves were also once foolish, disobedient, deceived, serving various lusts and pleasures, living in malice and envy, hateful and hating one another.

However, the blood of Jesus changed all that.

> But when the kindness and the love of God our Savior toward man appeared, not by works of righteousness which we have done,

but according to His mercy He saved us, through the washing of regeneration and renewing of the Holy Spirit, whom He poured out on us abundantly through Jesus Christ our Savior, that having been justified by His grace we should become heirs according to the hope of eternal life. This is a faithful saying, and these things I want you to affirm constantly, that those who have believed in God should be careful to maintain good works. These things are good and profitable to men (Titus 3:4-8).

When you believe in Jesus and are washed in His blood through baptism, everything changes. No longer are you associated with wicked things, even though the rest of the world (or island) around you is immersed in it. Instead, you are given over to a life of good works; works that will bring honor and glory to the One who saved you.

THE POINT

It is highly likely that the world around you, the very community you are living in, is filled with liars, evil beasts, and lazy gluttons. Sadly, there may even be idle talkers and deceivers within your congregation. Instead of letting these facts discourage you, let them propel you toward good works. After all, if Titus was your preacher, that's exactly what he would be telling you every Sunday. Maintain good works! Be a pattern of good works! Live a life that is wholly devoted to glorifying God!

The church in Galatia was experiencing some tumult of their own, with members of the congregation falling back into sin. To the faithful, Paul wrote, "let us not grow weary while doing good, for in due season we shall reap if we do not lose heart. Therefore, as we have opportunity, let us do good to all, especially to those who are of the household of faith" (Gal. 6:9-10). While there were backsliding Christians living lives that would have been discouraging to the faithful, they were encouraged to keep doing good, even if there was a great temptation to quit.

The question is, how?! How is it possible to not grow weary? How can we continually keep ourselves on fire for good works? The answer to that question is pretty much the answer to every question: keep your eyes fixed on the ultimate example.

In the sermon Peter delivered to Cornelius and his household, he told them that Jesus "went about doing good" (Acts 10:38). There's our pattern. Was it easy for Jesus to continuously go about doing good? Absolutely not! There were days when He didn't even have time to eat (Mark 3:20). While it wasn't always the most convenient path, it was an easy choice for our Lord, because doing good was doing the will of the Father.

There will be days when you just don't feel like doing good. Calling the person who hasn't been at services will feel like a chore. Paying for someone's meal will seem like a burden. Giving up time for one of your hobbies in order to participate in a service project might feel almost unbearable. On those days, realize that your flesh is trying to take control. Our flesh, which is tempted frequently by Satan, will want to stop doing good when it's inconvenient. Our flesh will want to stop doing good works when the people around us don't seem to appreciate them. Our flesh will want to quit, but our hearts – fixed on Jesus – will have to tell it no.

Remember, Jesus created you with the purpose of doing good works (Eph. 2:10). He died to redeem you from lawless deeds and turn you into His own special person who is zealous for good works (Titus 2:14). You can't let the world around you get you down. Paul realized that this might be a temptation, which is why he instructed Titus to tell the people living on Crete, who were surrounded by evil both without and within, to be a people of good works. And he didn't just tell them once, though that's all it would have taken; he told them five times! Five times in this little epistle, Paul encouraged them to maintain good works! He knew it wouldn't be easy, not while surrounded by such discouraging people. Still, it was necessary if they wanted to be people who were truly living a Christ-centered life.

Obviously this idea of good works is Biblical, yet sadly some people take it to an extreme to which it was never meant to be taken. Instead of doing good to bring glory and honor to the Father, they have perverted the idea of doing good into something by which we earn our salvation. Rather than doing their best to bring glory to God, some would pat themselves on the back for a job well done then sit back and think they deserve the rest that is promised in heaven. Twice in this short letter, Paul points out that a mindset like that is completely and utterly wrong.

First, in Titus 2:11, Paul points out that it is the "grace of God that brings salvation." In the second place, he elaborates by saying:

> when the kindness and the love of God our Savior toward man appeared, not by works of righteousness which we have done, but according to His mercy He saved us, through the washing of regeneration and renewing of the Holy Spirit, whom He poured out on us abundantly through Jesus Christ our Savior, that having been justified by His grace we should become heirs according to the hope of eternal life (3:4-7).

Notice that it is the kindness of God and not the works we have done that brought salvation. It is His mercy in giving us Jesus Christ that brings salvation, not anything we do. We do good works as a means of praising Him for our salvation, not as a means of earning our salvation!

So do good, not because it earns you a spot in heaven, but because God saved you from the destiny you deserved: hell! Do good so that others will praise and magnify His name. Do good so that others might see Him in you and come to know Him for themselves. Do good, not so people notice you, but so that people notice the difference in you. The Christians in Crete had the opportunity, through good works, to show the rest of the Cretans just what a difference Jesus Christ had made in their lives. No longer were they gluttons or liars; instead, they were "sober, righteous, and godly" in an ungodly world (Titus 2:12).

In our dark world, we can be the same beacon of light the Cretan Christians were if we will be a people who are dedicated to doing good. Even if it's hard. Even when it's inconvenient. Do good, and in so doing, give others the opportunity to see Jesus living in you.

⁓∞⁓

I: How have authors, journalists, and bloggers described the people in your area? Are these views accurate? How would you describe the climate in which you live?

II: What specific good works can you do to show Jesus to your community?

III: What specific good works can you do to encourage those in your congregation to glorify God?

IV: What specific good works can you do to encourage those in your family to glorify God?

V: Make a list of good works you can do this week to bring glory to God.

XI

EXPOSING DISTRESS
Rome

*When hardships come, do you respond
with praise or a pity-party?*

৵৵৽

As the first century's largest city, Rome had a population of approximately one million people. Established in 27 BC, the Roman empire took the world by storm, or rather, by literal force. Bringing nearly all of the regions of Europe, Asia, and even parts of Africa under their control, Rome's conquest was a thing of legend. They established roads and aqueducts which brought the world to a new level of sophistication. The empire truly was larger than life, and its emperors were worshiped as gods.

Though the language, art, and philosophies of the Hellenistic (Greek) culture would continue to permeate most of the Greco-Roman world, the city of Rome was entirely different. The common language was Latin, their outlook far less religious, and their tolerance for other ideologies was nearly nonexistent. In Rome, the emperor was god and loyalty to the empire was the religion. Anything that went against either of those two things would be punished, likely by death.

Surprisingly, Rome was not eager to dissolve all other religions. As long as the organizations weren't criminal and didn't pose a threat to the Roman lifestyle they would be left alone. However, if a religion crossed over into what Roman officials considered "civil matters" – like pledging loyalty to Christ over allegiance to Rome – then things were different. "The most serious charge brought against Christians, however, was simply that they refused to be loyal citizens and to prove their loyalty by performing ritual acts, whether they believed in them or not."[1] Because of these "acts of treason," as the Roman government interpreted it, Christians in Rome and the surrounding districts were severely persecuted.

One of the more gruesome emperors Rome ever had was a man named Nero, who ruled during the time that Christianity was experiencing rapid growth (54-68 AD.) Nero, for all intents and purposes, was a lunatic. Many scholars believe that his vices had driven him mad, to the point that in 64 AD he burned a portion of the capitol city. Not wanting to be blamed for such an incredulous act, Nero blamed a mostly hated group for the crime: Christians. Because of this false accusation, followers of Jesus were "covered in the pelts of wild animals, torn to death by dogs, or were crucified, or were set on fire as torches when the daylight had faded,"[2] Some also argue that Nero used the burning corpses of Christians to light his own gardens for special events, turning his false accusation from simply the torture of innocent people into a spectacle and sport for his depraved citizens to enjoy.

These types of executions would have been rather typical for a Roman citizen to encounter. After all, their most enjoyable form of entertainment was gathering around the Circus Maximus or Colosseum to watch bloody chariot races and deadly gladiator games. Romans cheered when criminals

---

[1] Bell, Albert A. *Exploring the New Testament World*. Nashville: T. Nelson, 1998. Print.

[2] Tacitus, *Annals*, 15.44

were executed in front of their very eyes. They lived for bloodshed and fighting. These were a callous and bloodthirsty people, and in the first century, their sights were set on a group of people who called themselves Christians.

THE PASSAGE

Paul had Roman citizenship, which was a coveted thing in the first century. Because of this, he had certain rights that could not be ignored. Thus, he was not swiftly put to death for being a Christian as others would have been. Instead, he was entitled to a trial, though we know ultimately Nero had him put to death. Still, Paul was granted an extension of life because of his Roman citizenship. This proved to be most beneficial to the church because he was able to write many letters while imprisoned in Rome.

At least eleven times throughout the New Testament, Paul referenced the chains he was in for Christ's sake, though he never used them as a source of complaint or excuse. Instead, it seems Paul's imprisonments only encouraged him. How is that even possible? How can one find joy and encouragement while being falsely imprisoned? It is because Paul saw his chains as an opportunity to magnify Christ.

But I want you to know, brethren, that the things which happened to me have actually turned out for the furtherance of the gospel, so that it has become evident to the whole palace guard, and to all the rest, that my chains are in Christ; and most of the brethren in the Lord, having become confident by my chains, are much more bold to speak the word without fear. For I know that this will turn out for my deliverance through your prayer and the supply of the Spirit of Jesus Christ, according to my earnest expectation and hope that in nothing I shall be ashamed, but with all boldness, as always, so now also Christ will be magnified in my body, whether by life or by death. For to me, to live is Christ, and to die is gain (Phi. 1:12-14, 19-21).

Paul had plenty about which to be discouraged. He had heard reports of those who had succumbed to Roman execution. Even his close friends, Aquila and Priscilla, had put their lives on the line for his sake (Rom. 16: 3-4). Beyond that, Paul was still haunted by his role in Stephen's death and the instrumental part he had once played in ripping Christians away from their families. However, Paul didn't let these things bring him down. Instead, he used the position he was in to bring others to Christ. He taught the guards who were charged with watching him. He wrote letters to congregations and individuals which urged them to remain strong in the Lord. Though his situation was less than ideal, he used the circumstances he found himself in to bring the most glory to God that he possibly could.

THE POINT

The Christian life is all about perspective. Because we live in a time where Christianity is growing less and less favorable in the eyes of the government and the majority of citizens, our perspective is going to be the key to our continued faithfulness. What if Paul had given up when he was put in prison? We wouldn't have the books of the Bible we know as Philippians, Ephesians, Colossians, or Philemon. The palace guard wouldn't have heard the message of Jesus, nor would those who visited him at his lodging in Rome (Acts 28:24). Paul accomplished so much good for the cause of Christ during his time of imprisonment, and that is because he maintained a heavenly perspective.

In Colossians 3:2, Paul, from prison, encouraged Christians to set their minds on things above. As those who have been washed in the blood of Jesus and cleansed from every sin, our minds can't be on the carnal anymore. Instead, we are to be seeking heavenly things, viewing life from an eternal perspective. The Hebrews writer tells us exactly how to do that: look to the One (and ones) who endured much more than you are currently experiencing.

> Therefore we also, since we are surrounded by so great a cloud of witnesses, let us lay aside every weight, and the sin which so easily ensnares us, and let us run with endurance the race that is set before us, looking unto Jesus, the author and finisher of our faith, who for the joy that was set before Him endured the cross, despising the shame, and has sat down at the right hand of the throne of God (Heb. 12:1-2).

First, we are instructed to think about the great cloud of witnesses that is pictured as "leaning over to watch us in the running of the race like the crowds in a great stadium who are watching the athletic events."[3] This "cloud of witnesses" is a multitude of God's faithful people who have experienced horrendous things. Hebrews 11:35-38 tells us more about these witnesses:

> "[they] were tortured, not accepting deliverance, that they might obtain a better resurrection. Still others had trial of mockings and scourgings, yes, and of chains and imprisonment. They were stoned, they were sawn in two, were tempted, were slain with the sword. They wandered about in sheepskins and goatskins, being

---

[3] Lenski, R.C.H. *Commentary on the New Testament.* Columbus, OH: Wartburg, 1942. Print.

destitute, afflicted, tormented – of whom the world was not worthy. They wandered in deserts and mountains, in dens and caves of the earth.

These people are the cheering crowd we are surrounded by on our Christian journey. They are not witnesses of our deeds, but are instead "witnesses whose life, works, sufferings, [and] death attest their own faith, testify to us through the pages of Holy Writ and in other history that they were true men of faith indeed."[4] They are people who suffered horrific things simply because they were following God, and their examples are to encourage us to keep on keeping on, even when the going gets tough. Should you become discouraged to the point that you feel like giving up, you are to remember all that these faithful men and women have done, and imagine looking them in the eye and telling them that you just can't take it anymore.

That is just the first example, though. Next, we are instructed to look to Jesus and all that He endured so that we could be in heaven with Him one day. Is your situation so terrible that you want to neglect the salvation Christ purchased with His own blood? Is what's happening to you so unimaginably hard that you could tell Jesus that what He went through wasn't worth it? We must let this great cloud of faithful witnesses and our very Lord and Savior Jesus Christ encourage us to keep on – to keep fighting – to run the race with endurance and long-suffering. Let Him encourage us to never, ever give up, because He didn't give up on us.

Sure, the apostle Paul faced some difficult things during his ministry, but it was nothing in comparison to what Christ went through to make salvation possible for His people. In fact, Paul said it wasn't anything at all in comparison to the joy of heaven that awaits those who endure to the end. But, how

[4] Ibid.

could he say that? Just look at the extensive list of difficulties Paul faced:

> From the Jews five times I received forty stripes minus one. Three times I was beaten with rods; once I was stoned; three times I was shipwrecked; a night and a day I have been in the deep; in journeys often, in perils of waters, in perils of robbers, in perils of my own countrymen, in perils of the Gentiles, in perils in the city, in perils in the wilderness, in perils in the sea, in perils among false brethren; in weariness and toil, in sleeplessness often, in hunger and thirst, in fastings often, in cold and nakedness-- besides the other things, what comes upon me daily: my deep concern for all the churches (2 Cor. 11:24-28).

According to Paul, these things were merely "light, momentary affliction" (2 Cor. 4:17). Paul could have this mindset because his perspective was a heavenly one. Instead of focusing on the negative things that happened to him on earth, Paul focused on the crown of life that awaited him in heaven (2 Tim. 4:7-8). Whatever you face, however bad it may seem, remember this: anything and everything we suffer is worth what heaven holds. And none of it holds a candle to what our sinless Lord endured on the cross – the cross that should have been occupied by you and me.

Roman Christians were tortured, humiliated, ripped away from their families, and some were even brutally murdered. When Satan attempts to discourage you, and tells you to give up, remember these brothers and sisters. You can have their faith and their victory if you will keep your eyes focused on Jesus.

の⊷⋖

I: List all of the things Paul endured for the cause of Christ (2 Cor. 11:24-28).

II: What types of negative circumstances in your life tempt you to become discouraged?

III: What two things does the Hebrews writer encourage us to think about when things are difficult (Heb. 12:1-2)?

IV: Write out Colossians 3:1-2 on a notepad and keep it beside your bed. Read it every night as you close out your day.

V: What things have you endured that are more difficult than what Christ endured for you?

XII

EXPOSING SEPARATION

Patmos

*Are your eyes fixed on Jesus
or on the present world?*

꥟◦◦꥟

The island of Patmos is located in the Aegean Sea approximately 65 miles off the coast of Ephesus and roughly 22 miles southwest of the island of Samos. The small island, a mere seven miles long, was used by the Romans "to banish political and religious enemies of the state."[1] The emperor Domitian, who ruled from 81-96 AD, was particularly known for frequently sending those in opposition to him or his empire to the volcanic island, especially those who would have had ties to Ephesus. It is no wonder, then, that the apostle John, about whom secular history tells us resided in the city of Ephesus, is banished to the island of Patmos for, or because of, "the word of God and for the testimony of Jesus Christ" (Rev. 1:9).

The island itself had a high, fortified acropolis that the Roman officials would have used to watch the inhabitants of the island as well as the sea traffic. There were temples to

---

[1] Wilson, Mark W. *Biblical Turkey; A Guide to the Jewish and Christian Sites of Asia Minor.* Istanbul, Turkey: Ege Yayinlari, 2010. Print.

Artemis and Aphrodite on the island as well, though not of the same magnitude that the mainland boasted.

Scholars are torn on what life on the island was actually like. Some, noting the rocky, sparse terrain, propose Patmos was used solely as a penal colony, while others claim the island had other small civilian colonies along the coastline. Because of this dispute, scholars also disagree on John's lifestyle while he was living in Patmos. Some suggest he was banished with hard labor, while others suggest he was merely sent to the island and was free to live in one of the coastal areas. Regardless of the view you choose to take, know this: John was exiled. He was forced away from his home and his church family in Ephesus and placed on a small, volcanic island for over a year. His view was sea, sea, and more sea. With only 13 square miles around which to wander, the landscape would have gotten old, regardless of whether he was free to roam or not.

Many scholars believe that Prochorus (Acts 6:5) was somewhat of a secretary to John, and that he was the one to carry the revelation to the seven churches. His route would have likely started by taking a boat from Patmos to the closest town, Miletus, and then traveling north on the Roman road that led to Ephesus, the first of the seven churches of Asia mentioned in the letter. From there, the letters in Revelation 2-3 are listed in geographical order. Traveling north, he would have come to Smyrna, then Pergamum, then headed southeast toward Thyatira. Continuing in a southeasterly direction, he would have come to Sardis, Philadelphia, and finally Laodicea. Once Prochorus had taken the revelation to all of the churches, he likely would have gotten on the Anatolian highway in Laodicea that would have taken him straight back to Ephesus.

After Domitian died in 96 AD, all of the prisoners he had exiled were released by Emperor Nerva. In keeping with the

95 AD dating of the book of Revelation that the majority of scholars hold, it seems John's exile would have only lasted approximately 18 months. Thus, he likely returned to Ephesus after being freed from Patmos, and was able to join his follow laborer Prochorus and his other brothers and sisters in the city.

THE PASSAGE

While John's exile would have been less than two years, it would not have been an easy time. One of the most difficult aspects of his banishment was the separation he had from everyone he loved. It is not surprising, then, that when John receives the revelation from Jesus Himself on that fateful Lord's Day (Rev. 1:10) he "fell at His feet as dead" (v. 17).

Jesus was one of John's very best friends, yet seeing the Christ in His exalted glory was too much for the lonely apostle to bear. While John would have traveled with Jesus for many years, studying at His feet and drinking in His every word, having Jesus appear to him in a vision on the island of Patmos overwhelmed him completely. No doubt a part of the reason was because John's exiled soul longed for companionship. He missed the days when he could worship with those of a kindred mind. He longed for the days when he walked by the sea with his dear Friend; especially now that the sea was his bitter enemy, separating him from all the ones he loved.

It seems John personifies separation in the form of the sea in Revelation 21. In that chapter, he began a discussion about heaven and how amazing it will be. Among the first things he listed was the fact that there would be "no more sea" (21:1). Why was this such a monumental part of heaven for John? Because heaven would be a place of no more separation – not from his brothers and sisters, and not from God. In heaven, he would be united around God's very throne with both his beloved Friend, Jesus, and with all those who had faced death at the hands of a cruel Roman empire.

In heaven, John would experience "no more death, nor sorrow, nor crying" (Rev. 21:4). How much sorrow and crying had John experienced on the island of Patmos? How much pain had he endured, banished and alone in the middle of the sea? Heaven, he noted, would be drastically different. Heaven would have no sorrow, no crying, no pain, and no separation. In heaven, he would forever be with God. It seems the book of Revelation was as encouraging and empowering for John himself as it was for those to whom he was writing.

THE POINT

Do you really want to go to heaven?

For a Christian, it may seem that the answer is obvious, but really think about it. Do you want to go to heaven? Do you long for it? Does it consume your mind? How often do you really sit and think about it? Be honest with yourself. How much time do you spend daydreaming of the moment you'll be face to face with the One who died for you? While it seems we know the right answer is to say that heaven is the place we most want to be and heaven is what we're living our whole life toward, it seems we neglect to really think about what that time will be like.

In Colossians 3:1, Paul had to tell the Christians in Colossae to "seek those things which are above, where Christ is, sitting at the right hand of God." As people who wear Jesus' name and have supposedly dedicated our entire lives to Him, why do we have to be told to think about where He is? Shouldn't that be a given? While it may seem that way, it's really not. Keeping your mind on heaven is hard work.

First of all, we've never been there. Though John paints

beautiful pictures in the book of Revelation, we don't know exactly what heaven will be like. Since we've never seen it or talked with anyone who has seen it, it's difficult to wrap our minds around really going there. Not to mention the fact that heaven is in a spiritual realm and our earthly minds can't comprehend that. Secondly, we're not there yet. We're on earth, and earth is distracting! It's filled with shiny things that take our attention off heaven and keep our minds solely focused on the here and now.

So how can we long for heaven? How can we keep our final destination at the forefront of our mind's eye? It starts with realizing that this world is not our home. To the Philippians, Paul wrote:

> For our citizenship is in heaven, from which we also eagerly wait for the Savior, the Lord Jesus Christ, who will transform our lowly body that it may be conformed to His glorious body, according to the working by which He is able even to subdue all things to Himself (Phi. 3:20-21).

Notice the two main points in this passage. First, your citizenship is in heaven. Earth is not home; it's your temporary dwelling. Paul told the Corinthians that life on earth is like living in a tent, but heaven is like living in a building – a permanent dwelling (2 Cor. 5:1). Have you ever been tent camping? I have, and it was rough! If you are anything like me, the entire time you're dwelling in the tent, you're thinking about being back home, living in a permanent structure that has glorious things like air-conditioning, running water, and a lack of bugs. This is what we are supposed to be doing on earth! Not dwelling on tent life. Not trying to turn our tents into immaculate dwellings. Instead, we are supposed to be desiring our permanent structure, heaven! That is where our true home, our citizenship, lies.

The second point Paul makes is this: you're supposed to be focused on Jesus. Jesus is in heaven preparing it for us right now (John 14:2-3). He is going to come back and take us to live with Him forever. Because He is there now and because He is preparing it for us, we should be "eagerly waiting" for Him, anxiously anticipating heaven!

It appears that one of the reasons we don't anticipate heaven like we should is because we don't think about Jesus enough. We get bogged down with everyday tent life that we kind of forget about Jesus. This is not only a terrible thing to do, it's also devastating to our spiritual health! If we don't think about Jesus as much as we should, we won't be faithful like we should. Why would we be? Reflecting on Jesus causes us to live lives dedicated to Him. Not thinking about Jesus leads us down a path where religion becomes ritual and our faith crumples beneath the weight of the very distracting, morally depraved world.

So think about Jesus. Really think about Him. Think about all He's done for you, in creating the world for you (Heb. 2:10) and going to the cross on your behalf. Think about all that He gave up in leaving heaven (His equality with God, for instance) only to be identified as a lowly human being (Phi. 2:5-8). Think about the glory He is in now, seated at the right hand of God, yet still pleading your case before Him as your advocate (1 John 2:1). When we spend time truly contemplating who Jesus is and what He has done, we'll understand more fully why John fell on his face in a prostrate position when the Lord appeared to him on Patmos (Rev. 1:17).

We should feel the effects of the separation from our Savior just as John felt the bitter loneliness the island of Patmos brought him. The more John thought of the sea (and he thought about it a lot: it's referenced more than twenty times in the book of Revelation), the more he longed for heaven. If we will spend more of our time thinking about Jesus and our separation from Him, we'll long more for heaven, too. Three times in Revelation 22 Jesus says He is "coming quickly" (v. 7, 12, 20). Does that thought terrify you or fill you with unbelievable joy and anticipation? If you don't think about Him frequently, it likely seems a bit scary. But if Jesus is our focus day in and day out – if going to heaven is truly our number one desire – we will be able to pray with the same fervor John did in Revelation 22:20 when he said, "Even so, come, Lord Jesus!"

John knew he didn't belong on the island of Patmos, so he spent his time thinking about heaven and how glorious it must be. You and I don't belong on earth; our citizenship is in heaven. So spend your time thinking about that beautiful place! Dwell on the place where our Savior is right this very moment; a place where there will be no more sea.

※

I: List John's description of heaven from Revelation 21:1-4. What are your favorite aspects of heaven?

II: Why is John's reference to 'no more sea' in Revelation 21:1 so important?

III: What analogies does Paul use to describe our earthly existence and our heavenly existence in 2 Corinthians 5:1?

IV: What parts of earthly life do you not enjoy? What parts of earthly life tempt you to forget your true home?

V: Set aside time to dwell on Jesus for 1-2 minutes every day. Set a reminder on your phone.

XIII

EXPOSING
THE ENEMY
Modern World

Will you let Satan win?

❧⋯❦

The modern world was established approximately 2,000 years after the New Testament era. After the fall of the Roman Empire in 476 AD, the world saw many tumultuous years in which many different kingdoms and countries sought world domination. This ebb and flow of war and peace continued all the way through 1945 AD, when the majority of the known world went to war, seeking to stop German dictator Adolf Hitler from taking control. When he was defeated, the world saw a time of peace. Toward the end of 1945, nearly all the great powers of the world aligned themselves under what would be called the United Nations (UN).

Through the establishment of the UN, each country possessed its own borders and regulatory powers, so long as those powers did not interfere with the peace of other countries. While there have been times of unrest since 1945, the modern world is still enjoying a time of relative peace, and most countries are even thriving.

The prosperity of nations today likely exceeds that of any previous generations of peoples. Medical advancements, technological breakthroughs, and widespread abilities for communication have changed nearly every aspect of life for the residents of the modern world. The effects of such advancements, while one would assume would be favorable, have actually taken the world's moral compass in a southerly direction.

In the modern world, the residents often make depravity entertainment. Multiple theaters are found in nearly every city and sexually-charged scenes dominate the screens. People do not even have to leave their homes anymore to enjoy such entertainment, as televisions and computers bring scenes of pornography, adultery, homosexuality, and fornication right into their very living spaces. With an abundance of sexual deviancy pressing on every side, it is no wonder that the inhabitants of the modern world have chosen to embrace such lifestyles instead of finding them shameful. Homosexuality is not only accepted, it is celebrated. Adultery is nearly a foreign concept because divorce for any number of reasons, including simply "irreconcilable differences", is the common practice.

With the makeup of the home shaken by a lack of respect for marriage and sexual purity, there is no "normal" family makeup for modern world residents. Instead, the majority of families are disjointed, leaving children with perhaps only one parent, or maybe two parents of the same gender. These children are encouraged to choose for themselves what gender they want to be, because the modern world sees things such as genetic makeup as very fluid and free. Of course, many children are not even given the chance to grow up in the modern world, with the legalization of abortion killing over a million children every year in the United States alone.

Another area of interest in the modern world is the worship of celebrities and athletes. Devotees gather in temples known as arenas and align themselves under a certain team or artist. This usually costs a substantial amount of money and requires a great deal of time and dedication. However, artists and athletes aren't the only individuals under whom people align themselves. In the name of religion, many in the modern world are divided under different men. Some follow after Martin Luther, some a man known as the pope, others under a man named Muhammad, and others still under a variety of different names.

While it seems the modern world is at peace, truly there is turmoil bubbling from within in the form of moral decay. Should it continue down this path, there is no telling how long the modern world will continue to stand.

THE PASSAGE

While the New Testament writings were concluded by the end of the first century, the apostle Paul had plenty to say about the modern world.

> But know this, that in the last days perilous times will come: For men will be lovers of themselves, lovers of money, boasters, proud, blasphemers, disobedient to parents, unthankful, unholy, unloving, unforgiving, slanderers, without self-control, brutal, despisers of good, traitors, headstrong, haughty, lovers of pleasure rather than lovers of God, having a form of godliness but denying its power. And from such people turn away! (2 Tim. 3:1-5).

While disturbing, truly the modern world fits this description. Perhaps working backward in the text shows the true extent of the problems with the world today.

First, men have a form of godliness but deny its power. Many claim to know God, to have a relationship with Him, and to worship Him regularly. The truth of the matter is, few people know God and have a relationship with Him. Instead, they simply cling to the idea of God, and even then only when it is convenient for them. Even "in so-called Christian lands the world, too, adopts many Christian forms... in having prayers offered on all sorts of occasions, in talking about God, religion, morality. But where is 'the power thereof,' the divine, spiritual, regenerating, renewing, saving power of Christ and the true gospel? Totally absent."[1] Having a form of godliness is really like having no godliness at all.

Instead of truly honoring God in every action and thought, the modern world's inhabitants have become "lovers of pleasure rather than lovers of God." Though the modern world has access to God's entire revealed will, something previous generations would be quite envious of, they choose pleasure rather than truth. They choose to go after their own fleshly desires, loving themselves far more than they love God. Because of this, they become all of the things Paul spoke about in 2 Timothy 3:1-4. When self comes first and God comes next (or last or isn't even on the radar), people become proud, unthankful, headstrong, brutal, and without self-control. People get lost, really lost, from the Way about which Jesus spoke, and instead merrily skip down the broad path that leads to destruction.

When people behave like this, and people are behaving like this, Paul would call it "perilous times." That word perilous literally means harsh or difficult. For those who are truly seeking to follow God and love Him with their entire being, it is going to be difficult living in such a harsh climate, surrounded on every side with wickedness and moral decay. Such is the life of a modern day Christian. They reside in a world that claims to have some semblance of Christianity and moral goodness, yet the reality is that the world they live in is perilous and in danger of rapid decay.

---

[1] Lenski, R.C.H. *Commentary on the New Testament*. Columbus, OH: Wartburg, 1942. Print.

THE POINT

While 2,000 years have passed from the time of the New Testament world, very little has really changed. People still worship false gods, are involved in every kind of wickedness and sexual depravity, and are filled with pride and greed. Though millennia gives a lot of time for learning from and correcting past mistakes, our world has become exactly what the apostle Paul said it would in 2 Timothy 3:7, filled with a people who are "always learning and never able to come to the knowledge of the truth."

"[T]he Roman Empire fell slowly, as a result of challenges from within and without, and changing over the course of hundreds of years until its form was unrecognizable"[2]. This is exactly the path that the modern world has ventured down. Intellectually, we know that many modern countries were founded with religion at the heart of their government, but to look at the current state of the world we live in would make you scratch your head and wonder how we got so far from morality and decency. The answer is simple: a world where God doesn't rule is a world where morality and decency fall by the wayside.

Ultimately, though, the world has always been this way. There has always been idolatry and self-worship. People have always put "stuff" on a pedestal; placing things above people and especially above God. The world has always felt self-reliant; thinking it was wealthy enough to take care of itself and provide for itself, when the reality was that they were poor, blind, and naked. These boastful thoughts have always left the world unguarded and vulnerable to Satan's attacks; his

---

[2] Gill, N.S. "The Fall of Rome: How, When and Why Did It Happen?" ThoughtCo. March 13, 2018. https://www.thoughtco.com/what-was-the-fall-of-rome-112688

penetration of their hearts leading them to be liars, evil beasts, and lazy gluttons. And because this is the way the world has always been, Christians have always had a hard time living in the world.

Because Christians are called to be separate from the world – not conforming to its lusts and evil desires and lack of morals – they have always had an uphill battle. Disciples of Jesus have always been in the minority, fighting against Satan's seemingly never-ending, ever-increasing forces. While this has always been the case, one fact has always been true: God is greater than the devil.

In 1 John 4:4, John tells his readers, "He who is in you is greater than he who is in the world." So the world is full of sexually depraved, morally bankrupt, sin-corrupted people? So those people are vocal, criticizing anyone who would speak against their chosen lifestyle? So sin is becoming more and more widely accepted, even among those who would claim a semblance of Christianity? So, what? God is still greater, and He will reward those who endure to the end.

If we will devote ourselves to good works, undeterred by persecution or personal excuses, God will deliver us. If we will truly separate ourselves from the world and become the holy people He has called us to be, our Father will give us the salvation He's promised! It won't be an easy journey, our time here in a sin-filled world, but it will be worth it. Seeing Jesus in His exalted glory will be worth it. Spending eternity in heaven with the God of the universe will be worth it. Being delivered from pain and sickness and death and separation will make the light, momentary afflictions we've gone through on this earth worth it.

Satan is not going to give up, though. He has been perfecting his lies and deceptions for thousands of years. Two things in particular are going to get in our way when it comes to living a godly life. The first is the temptation to conform. When it seems like everyone around you is wicked, sometimes the thought of 'why should I' pops into our heads. Why should I get up on Sunday morning and worship God, when half the people in attendance don't even want to be there? Why should I go out of my way to tell others about Jesus, when they don't even want to hear it anyway? Why should I abstain from fulfilling my sexual appetite, when the rest of the world encourages it? Why should I give up drinking or drugs, when the world tells me to do whatever makes me happy? Why should I follow the Bible so closely, when the world says it's just an outdated book anyway? Why should I follow only after Christ, when the rest of the world doesn't seem to mind that they're aligned under fallible men?

The world will constantly press upon your heart. These thoughts and a thousand more will seek to creep into your mind and overtake it. Just know that this is Satan, launching those fiery darts in your direction. When those thoughts come up, remember, "He who is in you is greater than He who is in the world" (1 John 4:4).

The second thing that is going to try to hinder us on our journey is persecution. Paul told us that "all who desire to live godly in Christ Jesus will suffer persecution," yet two verses later he said, "but you must continue" (2 Tim. 3:12, 14). The temptation to quit will be there. If you are faced with the choice between God or death, you will be tempted to choose self-preservation. But know that living a godly life is the choice we must continually make, regardless of how difficult it becomes. Choosing to be faithful to God, regarldess of the earthly outcome, is true self-preservation!

I once heard someone say, "God is more intent on perfecting you through trials than protecting you from them." If your aim is to live a life modeled after Christ, you will suffer. After all, isn't that the life He led? Didn't He suffer much at the hands of both the Jews and the Romans? Still, He was faithful to God and His will, and you and I must do the same. When hardships come because we believe in and stand up for Jesus, keep holding on, and remember that you are not alone (Heb. 12:1).

The Christians in the first century world faced these same temptations. The temptation to conform would have been huge, especially when everyone they knew was headed to a temple to participate in a sexually-charged feast in honor of a so-called god. They would have wanted to give in when members of the congregation were continuing to practice sexual immorality and other forms of ungodliness. They would have been tempted to let their wealth puff them up like it did their neighbors, but this wasn't acceptable. None of these thoughts were acceptable. They were to be holy, called out from their perverse generation, and so are we.

Ultimately, a first century Christian's refusal to conform would have led to extreme persecution. In some instances, failure to conform (to, say, bowing down to the emperor of Rome as if he were a god) would lead to their imprisonment or death. Still, they were to remain strong. Even when their freedoms were taken away, they were to be a people who were fully dedicated to their Lord. You and I are called to the same standard. Whatever our faith in Christ brings to us, we accept. Should it mean jail, we still hold true to Christ's message. Should it mean death, we remain faithful until the end. Regardless of what comes our way because of our dedication to Jesus Christ, we remain "steadfast, unmovable, and always abounding in the work of the Lord" (1 Cor. 15:58).

You would think the world would learn from the lessons of the past, but they continue to repeat the same mistakes as previous generations. That's fine. The world will always be the world. Just remember that you, Christian, are to always be holy. You are to always be different. No matter how far the world goes, no matter how bad things get, you are to remain true to

God and His commandments, continually seeking His counsel and His approval. What the world thinks doesn't matter. What the world participates in doesn't matter. What matters is your dedication to Christ. Regardless of your culture, hold fast to your Lord.

⁂

I: In what ways is the modern world just like the New Testament world?

II: What types of things do you think the modern world idolizes?

III: How do you think the present world relates to Paul's description to Timothy in 2 Timothy 4:3-4?

IV: In what ways are you tempted to conform to the world?

V: Which is a greater temptation for you when facing persecution: giving up or complaining?

ACKNOWLEDGMENTS

First, I want to thank my incredibly talented husband, **Robert**, for everything. Your support, encouragement, cover design, book layout, promotional video, and self-publishing expertise made all the difference. This book wouldn't exist without you.

To my daughter, **Anna**: Thank you for finally being a good napper. I couldn't have edited this without your cooperation.

To my editors, **Jessica Donovant**, **Christy Jenkins**, and **Emily Nelson**: Thank you for making sense of so many errors.

To **Brad McNutt**: Thank you for being the first outsider to read these words. Your feedback changed the way I approached the descriptions of the places.

As much as it pains me to say it, thank you to **Michael Whitworth** for answering hundreds of book-related questions.

And finally, to **Dr. Terry Edwards**: Your course on Paul's epistles inspired me to travel and to investigate first century life.

The Light Network
www.thelightnetwork.tv

Christian podcasts that will encourage your soul,
enlighten your mind, and empower your faith.

Wifey Wednesdays

Podcast Hosted by Emily Hatfield

Listen online at **TheLightNetwork.tv**

GET IT ON **Google Play**

Listen on **Apple Podcasts**

The Light Network
www.thelightnetwork.tv

OTHER PODCASTS BY EMILY HATFIELD

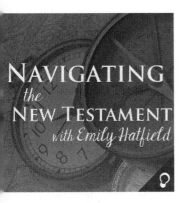

Emily's love of travel and passion for God's Word are combined in this show for ladies. Each episode features a different site with Emily's personal photos and an exploration of the accompanying Biblical text.

This show is available in both audio and video formats.

❧◦❧

This is a show designed with God's women in mind as they go about living their lives as members of the royal family of God. Each episode parallels a story about the British Monarchy with God's Royal Family.

There are 100 episodes online!

emilyhat.com

If you are looking for a place to find relatable, easy to understand content about God and His Word, *emilyhat.com* is a place for you. The goal for this website is to develop a two-sided relationship; one where the reader will feel free to contact Emily, ask her Biblical questions, and encourage her as she attempts to encourage you.

Above all, *emilyhat.com* serves as a means to point people to God, the Source of any wisdom you may gain through visiting the site. To Him all glory and honor is due.

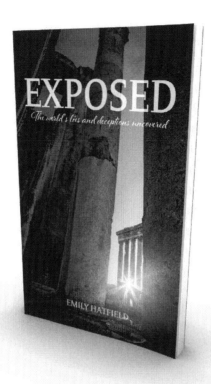

Order additional copies from . . .

The Light Network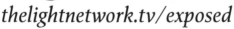
thelightnetwork.tv/exposed

Great for personal study, ladies devotionals,
or classroom study.

Paperback – $9.95
Ebook – $6.95

Orders of 20 or more will receive a bulk discount.

Made in the USA
Columbia, SC
18 July 2023

20461289R00083